ALL YOU NEED TO KNOW...

STALIN

BY CLAIRE SHAW

CONTENTS

For Grandma

10 9 8 7 6 5 4 3 2 1

ISBN 978-1-911187-89-9

First published as *All you need to know: Stalin*
by Connell Publishing in 2018

Picture credits:
Cover illustration © NatBasil / Shutterstock

Design: Ben Brannan
Associate Publisher: Paul Woodward
Edited by Jolyon Connell
Assistant Editor and typeset by Alfred Fletcher

Printed in Great Britain

INTRODUCTION

We all know Stalin; or at least, we think we do. The Georgian student priest who grew up to be one of the twentieth century's most notorious mass-murderers is the subject of countless books and documentaries, his plans and policies appearing on the curriculum of thousands of school pupils. Since his death in 1953, historians have picked over his biography and rehashed the major features of his leadership, tracing his radicalisation, his growing paranoia and his murderous intentions, all concealed by the glorious façade of his personality cult.

Look a little closer, however, and the easy narrative collapses. Like the country he led, Stalin can be seen, to borrow Churchill's phrase, as a 'riddle wrapped in a mystery inside an enigma'. This is partly to do with the enormity of the crimes he committed, which tend to preclude easy analysis. As Sheila Fitzpatrick, one of the most prolific and influential historians of the Stalin era, has pointed out, "'Absolute evil' is not a useful concept, at least from point of view of a biographer'. Stalin the man is entwined in a complicated fashion with Stalinism, the political system that developed under his rule, which is either a perversion of the socialist experiment or the worst excesses of it, depending on one's point of view. Very few political regimes have been personalised in such a way (Nazism does not bear the name of Hitler, for example). As a result, it is difficult to disentangle the results of his policies from their intentions, or to consider Stalin's political career with an objective eye. Some troubling questions remain: What visions underpinned his actions? What policies and practices enabled him to rule for so long? Why did nobody stop him?

Sources for untangling these questions are many. While Stalin left no memoirs or diaries – unlike some of his fellow dictators – his articles and theoretical works give a good sense of his developing ideology and the trends of his political thinking. Contemporary accounts by Stalin's friends and colleagues have lent colour and personality to more recent biographies, most notably the two volumes by Simon Sebag-Montefiore. Since the collapse of the USSR and the opening of the archives, it has been possible to trace Stalin's involvement in the workings of government; these sources have recently been used to great effect in biographies by Oleg Khlevniuk and Stephen Kotkin. While there is much more material to be mined, most historians do not anticipate any sensational new revelations about Stalin's life. Yet biographies of Stalin continue to be written and hotly debated, fictionalised accounts of the period continue to appear, and the news cycle continues to react instantly to stories of the dictator.

Why do we continue to care about Stalin? For one thing, his political career encompassed one of the most turbulent periods in modern history. Within his lifetime, Russia and her neighbours endured a series of violent revolutions, two world wars, the forced collectivisation of agriculture, a major industrialisation drive, and the violent cataclysms of the Purges, when millions were executed or imprisoned as 'enemies of the people'. A vast social experiment was launched to radically remake the nature of human society on the basis of equality and the redistribution of wealth; its implementation resulted in a violent and coercive regime that had little respect for human life or the natural world. Stalin did not create this political vision; he walked in the footsteps of other leaders and thinkers, such as Marx, Lenin and Trotsky, who fundamentally shaped his world view. His interpretation of Marxist thought was radically different from his Bolshevik predecessors, however, setting the USSR on a new and complicated path. Stalin thus needs to be understood as both an architect and a product of Soviet socialism.

Stalin's rule was eventful, but this is not the only reason the history of his leadership continues to hold sway. His is also a personal history, and a history of personality. Stalin's role as *vozhd* (leader) cannot be understood without considering his charisma, his ability to persuade and his hold over those around him. At the same time, biographies continue to grapple with the question of his ill-health, his paranoia, his wife's suicide, and the extent to which these factors influenced his policies. The monstrous nature of his actions later in life, and the way in which he promoted his own glorious public persona, are infinitely fascinating; like watching a horror film, we find it hard to look but cannot look away. Unlike many of those writing during the Soviet era, however, we do so from a position of relative security and freedom. We were not touched by his regime, and thus we can debate its excesses in safety.

For this reason, however, unpicking the issues of his leadership is vitally important. As much as Stalin's 'evil' is repellent, the seductiveness of his ideas still remains apparent, both in Putin's Russia, where nostalgia for Stalin's 'strong hand' continues to grow, and elsewhere. The system he built still influences policy in North Korea and Communist China. Historians now seek to explain the excesses of his leadership, not simply as an accident of personality, but also as the product of a particular historical context. Such is the nature, they argue, of great ideological visions, particularly in the context of major social upheavals. Stalin's actions are undeniably horrific, but they are significant not because he was a monster, but because he was all too human. Robert Service, in his biography of Stalin, asserts:

> Stalin carried out campaigns of carnage which have been described with words outside the lexicon of our species: monstrous, fiendish, reptilian; but the lesson to be learned from studying several of the twentieth century's most murderous politicians is that it is wrong to depict them as being wholly incomparable to ourselves. Not only wrong: it is also dangerous. If the likes of Stalin, Hitler, Mao Tse-tung and Pol Pot are represented as having been 'animals', 'monsters' and 'killing machines', we shall never be able to discern their successors.[1]

CHAPTER ONE

FROM DZHUGASHVILI TO STALIN

Historians have made much of Stalin's transition from Soso Dzhugashvili, the angel-faced Georgian seminary student, to Stalin, the murderous dictator. Yet sources regarding his early life are thin, and memoirs have not been able to escape the shadow of hindsight regarding his later role as revolutionary and totalitarian *vozhd*. Certainly, as the Russian historian Oleg Khlevniuk says, most biographers of Stalin have concentrated on tales of 'the childhood and youth of a future dictator, not the early years of Ioseb Jughashvili'.[2] His early life contains plenty of potential explanations for his bloody political career: his problematic family, his supposed Caucasian propensity to violence, and his political radicalisation. All are plausible, yet none is entirely satisfactory.

Iosef Vissarionovich Dzhugashvili was born in the Georgian

town of Gori, in the outskirts of the Russian Empire, on 6th December 1878 (though he would later officially change the date to 21st September 1879). His early family life was far from stable. His mother, Ekaterina (Keke), was the daughter of serfs; his father, Vissarion (Beso), was a cobbler. Iosef (known to the family as Soso) was their third child, their first two children having died in infancy. He was a delicate child who was frequently ill. At the age of seven, he contracted smallpox, which scarred his face and earned him the nickname 'Pockmarked'. As a schoolchild, he was struck in the street on two separate occasions by a phaeton; as a result of these unlucky accidents he was left with a limp and a permanently damaged left arm. Such misfortunes were compounded by his family situation. Beso's drinking habit, which developed in his son's infancy, caused him to lose the shoemaking business; both parents would regularly beat the young boy. Beso also spread rumours of Keke's infidelity and his son's illegitimacy: in later years, the rumoured candidates for Stalin's father would include a merchant, a priest, and even Tsar Alexander III himself.

While it is tempting to read this tale of deprivation and violence as the root of Stalin's 'distrust, alertness, evasion, dissimulation and endurance',[3] the situation was rather more complex. As Stephen Kotkin has argued, the trope of the traumatic childhood 'is too pat, even for those *with* traumatic childhoods'.[4] Unusually for the time, both Dzhugashvili's parents were literate. For Keke, in particular, education offered a path of upward mobility for her son, and she used every influence in Gori society to gain Dzhugashvili a spot at the local Theological School. Indeed, the young Stalin was a keen scholar, excelling in religious knowledge, languages (including Russian and Church Slavonic) and geography.

He sang beautifully and read the liturgy well, and was awarded a mark of 'excellent' for behaviour. There was an unfortunate incident in 1890, when Beso, who had by this time abandoned the family home, removed the young Stalin from school and enrolled him as an apprentice cobbler in Tiflis (now Tbilisi). Thanks to Keke's influence in the Georgian Orthodox Church, her son was quickly returned to his studies, graduating successfully in 1894. So far, so ordinary.

Those looking to Stalin's childhood for answers have also pointed to his country of birth as a possible explanation for his later behaviour. His contemporaries (and victims) certainly thought his Georgian identity significant. Lev Trotsky, in his damning condemnation of Stalin, made it clear that his place of birth was an important clue to the man he would become: he began his account of Stalin's life by speaking of the 'blending of grit, shrewdness, craftiness and cruelty which has been considered characteristic of the statesmen of Asia'. Nikolai Bukharin referred to him bitterly as 'Genghis Khan', a reference to the brutal Mongol leader who exercised control over Russia during the 13th century, calling up age-old notions of violence, ruthlessness and the essential 'foreignness' of Central Asia and the Caucasus to Russians.

For many historians, too, the notion of Georgia as part of the Russian 'borderlands', a contested space subject to oppression and domination by Russia, has been seen to explain Stalin's ruthless, elemental character. As Khlevniuk points out, however, the Russian Empire at the turn of the century was one vast borderland: "between Asia and Europe, between the promises of modernisation and the deteriorating traditional ways of life, between the city and the country, between authoritarianism and democratic strivings, between the obscurantism of the regime and the blood-thirstiness of many revolutionaries."[5]

In this light, it is difficult to lay all Stalin's crimes at Georgia's door. Rather more plausibly, Stalin's passionate conversion to Marxism is seen by Simon Sebag-Montefiore as deeply influenced by his identity as Georgian; Marx's tales of the oppression of the proletariat struck a chord with those who experienced the oppression of minority nationalities under the Russian empire's strict policies of Russification (the use of Russian language and traditions in all public institutions).

Identifying the roots of Stalin's character in his family life and national identity relies on a certain amount of supposition. Real

A modern map showing Georgia and south-west Asia

evidence of his developing rebellion came from his secondary education and exposure to Marxism. If Stalin displayed little inclination to rebel in Gori, let alone to involve himself in activity, the picture began to change when he enrolled in the Tiflis Theological Seminary. He had won a scholarship to the seminary, including free room and board, on the basis of his academic achievements. In his first year, he continued to achieve outstanding marks. Yet the strict and repressive policies of the seminary, which included surveillance, frequent searches and violent punishment, pushed the young seminarian towards revolt. This was not unusual; in fact, the seminary had briefly closed in the year before Stalin's enrolment after the students went on strike and demanded the end to arbitrary abuses of power by some of the teachers. In 1931, he would recall that 'in protest against the outrageous regime and the Jesuitical methods prevalent at the seminary, I was ready to become, and actually did become, a revolutionary'. He began secretly to borrow books from the city library, avidly reading Victor Hugo, Charles Darwin and Marx, learning of the romance of revolution, the death of God, and the leading role of the proletariat. He assumed leadership of an illegal reading group, his grades began to drop, and he was frequently punished for violating the rules.

Marxism clearly had a powerful attraction for the young would-be-revolutionary. As he later put it, his reading led him to the belief that 'the revolutionary proletariat alone is destined by history to liberate mankind and bring the world happiness'. This was far from unusual at this moment in history; Marxism was extraordinarily popular in the Russian Empire in the late 19th century, driven by the social and political upheavals of the country's rapid industrialisation process. The 'total' world view put forward by Marxism, with its faith in the inexorable progress of human history and the coming of socialism, was not that distant from the certainties of Orthodox Christianity; indeed, Yuri Slezkine has recently compared the Russian revolutionary movement to a 'millenarian sect'. Certainly, Stalin found his skills at reading the liturgy transferred easily to political meetings. His radicalism soon outgrew the seminary grounds. His desire to involve himself in 'real' politics led him to join a local branch of the Social Democratic Workers' Party, an underground network of Marxist organisations that had been formally founded in Minsk in 1898. Stalin's official biography describes his involvement with a local organisation of railway workers, for whom he acted as an unofficial propagandist and organiser. In 1899, when he was expelled from the seminary, his path as a Marxist revolutionary was already established.

These three strands – family, nationality and political ideology – play out in Stalin's experimentation with his name. It was during his time at the Tiflis Seminary that Soso, the diminutive form of Iosef, began to give way to more romantic pseudonyms. As a young seminarian, he published several poems with a local newspaper under the name Soselo. As his radicalism increased, he began to ask his comrades to call him Koba, the name of the hero of Georgian writer Alexander Kazbegi's novel *The Patricide*; his closest confidantes would continue to use that name throughout his life. The revolutionary movement was built on such pseudonyms, which had the practical purpose of concealing the identity of radicals from the tsarist Secret Police, yet the undeniable romance of choosing an alter ego, and projecting a new character to the world, clearly appealed to the young radical. His lasting pseudonym of Stalin did not emerge until 1913, with the publication of his first major Marxist ideological tract. Some historians have suggested that the name derived from that of his then lover, Liudmila Stal'. In the crucible of the revolution, however, its more literal meaning – 'the steel one', in the cosmopolitan language of Russian – gave Stalin the gravitas needed to assume his leading role.

Stalin's mother, Keke Geladze (1858 – 1937)

CHAPTER TWO

STALIN THE REVOLUTIONARY

Debates rage about the role Stalin played in the overthrow of tsarism and its replacement with the world's first socialist state. In his memoir of the Russian revolution, Nikolai Sukhanov dismissed Stalin's involvement, famously commenting that Stalin 'gave me the impression ... of a grey blur which flickered obscurely and left no trace'. Trotsky painted a similar picture of a man on the periphery, destined 'to always play second or third fiddle'. Stalin's official biography, by contrast, recounts that 'Lenin and Stalin inspired and organised the victory of the great October socialist revolution. Stalin was Lenin's closest associate. He directly managed all aspects of the preparation for the insurrection'. This narrative is so self-congratulatory that it is tempting to dismiss it out of hand. Recent histories have shown that the reality was somewhere in between. Stalin had the career of a fairly typical underground revolutionary, but one who combined a unique set of skills: those of fixer, propagandist and revolutionary theorist.

Russia at the turn of the twentieth century was in the grip of a revolutionary upsurge, driven by a widespread hatred of its authoritarian rulers. The Russian Empire was an absolute monarchy, in which all lands, lives and property belonged to the Tsar, and his word was akin to the word of God. This absolute rule sat awkwardly with an increasingly modern, educated and diverse Russian populace. Attempts to enact populist reforms in the 1860s, including the abolition of serfdom and introduction of trial by jury, had only succeeded in stoking rebellion; a popular terrorist wave led by an organisation called The People's Will ended with the assassination of Tsar Alexander II in 1881. The loss of one tsar did not change the system, however, and his successors were determined that their autocracy would not be limited.

Having failed to terrorise, Russian radicals turned to working-class politics. The industrialisation drive of the 1890s had produced a small, but increasingly radicalized, working class, who reacted against the terrible working conditions in the major cities by calling for labour protections and the right to unionise. This push for change was fomented and ultimately led by the Russian Social Democratic Workers' Party (RSDWP), an underground, Marxist organisation that aimed to bring about a workers' revolution in Russia. The nature of the coming revolution was a matter of some debate, however, and in 1903, the Party split in two. The majority (Bolshevik) faction were supporters of Lenin (the revolutionary name of Vladimir Il'ich Ulianov), who argued that the

Party had an obligation to lead the workers, acting as a vanguard and taking steps to accelerate the coming of revolution.

The minority (Menshevik) faction, on the other hand, believed that revolution would occur in its own time, and that they should take their cues from the workers and peasants themselves. Regardless of the tactical debates, this new form of revolutionary politics, including strikes and demonstrations, started to gain traction. In 1905, a general strike in St Petersburg led to an armed uprising that shut down the city and forced the tsar to make concessions, leading to the establishment of a parliament, or 'Duma'. For Lenin, this was only the beginning; as he commented in 1906, 'the movement is steadily rising towards ever more determined, offensive forms of struggle against the autocracy, forms that are assuming an increasingly mass character and are embracing the whole country'.

Stalin's main role in the chaotic early years of the movement was that of a tactician, corresponding with comrades in the centre to organise illegal strikes and demonstrations across Georgia. These events were often violent: in March 1902, troops opened fire on strikers in Batumi and thirteen people were killed. In the early 1900s, Stalin travelled across Georgia (in between several periods of imprisonment and exile), using his printing press to disseminate underground newspapers and establish new militant groups. In 1907, Stalin participated in his most infamous act of revolutionary banditry: an armed robbery in Tiflis, in which a group of revolutionaries from across the Caucasus stole 250,000 roubles from a local bank to fill the Bolshevik coffers. Several lives were lost, but this was not unusual; as Lenin had argued, violence and 'guerrilla warfare' were 'an inevitable form of struggle' at this stage in the revolutionary movement.

This was something of a controversial position, however, and many within the movement (particularly on the Menshevik side) disapproved of such overtly criminal acts. Stalin was considered *persona non grata* in Tiflis for several years following the robbery. Reading accounts of this period, one gets the sense that Stalin was already more violent and vindictive than most; his first murder, of a police spy, allegedly occurred in 1901.

Alongside his underground organisational activities, Stalin was increasingly valued by those in the Party as a propagandist. To be sure, he was never as charismatic an orator as Lenin or Trotsky. Robert Service describes his 'extraordinary polemical crudity' [6] and the dry content of his speeches, which he declaimed in a thick Georgian accent. Yet those in the underground valued his charisma and his plain speaking, giving him the nickname 'the Priest'. In prison, he organised readings and gave lectures to his fellow prisoners. He wrote and distributed political pamphlets to spread Bolshevik ideas. In the Georgian underground, he edited two newspapers, the Baku Proletariat and The Whistle; Sebag-Montefiore describes him in the thick of action during the Batumi strike, rushing to save his printing press and transport it to safer quarters. It is perhaps unsurprising that, in the upheavals of 1917, the editorship of the Party's central newspaper, *Pravda*, fell to him.

Stalin was also gaining popularity as a Marxist thinker in his own right. His first significant addition to Bolshevik Party theory came in 1913, with the publication of his *Marxism and the National Question*. Building on his position as the key Caucasian party member, Stalin put forward the notion that the minority

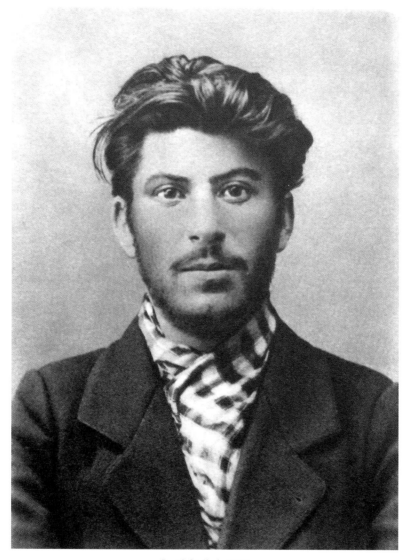

Joseph Stalin in 1902

nationalities within the Russian Empire were natural allies of the
proletariat, due to their oppression at the hands of the Russian
state, and should therefore be offered sovereignty and recognition
of their cultures as a means to attract them to the revolutionary

struggle. This work raised Stalin in Lenin's estimation – Lenin referred to it as 'really splendid' – and Stalin's views on minority nationalities would become central to Bolshevik policy before and after the revolution.

Meanwhile, he played an ever more dominant role in the political side of the underground movement. Like most revolutionaries, he spent the early 1900s in a protracted game of cat-and-mouse with the Okhrana, the tsarist Secret Police. Revolutionary activity – indeed, all political opposition – was strictly illegal under the tsarist regime, and the Okhrana worked to uncover plots against the Tsar, opening letters, tailing individuals, infiltrating organisations and keeping meticulous files on conspirators. For those they caught, the punishments varied, but most often took the form of administrative exile to Siberia. One notable exception was Lenin's older brother, Aleksandr Ulianov, whose execution for planning to assassinate Tsar Alexander III was a key moment in Lenin's own radicalisation. Stalin himself spent extended periods in prison and in exile in Siberia (in 1902-4, 1908-9, 1910-11 and 1913-17). These encounters with the Okhrana cemented his revolutionary idealism, and shaped his understanding of the nature of state power.

Stalin was first arrested in Batumi, following his masterminding of workers' disturbances there in 1902; he was imprisoned for 18 months before being exiled to Siberia. After a year, he managed to slip past the Okhrana and travel back to Tiflis. As Simon Sebag-Montefiore has shown, Stalin became notorious for these escapes, racking up nine arrests, four detentions and eight escapes in his underground career. Such escapes were not particularly hard to pull off, with a little planning and inventiveness. Siberian exiles were not physically imprisoned; it was believed that their distance from civilization was enough to protect ordinary Russian citizens from their influence. But Stalin had a particular talent for getting away. During his escape from Siberia, for example, he told the local policeman who arrested him that he was a member of the Okhrana – and persuaded the policeman to arrest the Okhrana agent who was on his tail instead.

This flair for escapology persuaded some contemporaries that Stalin himself served as a double agent for the Okhrana. Accusations emerged after his escape from exile in 1909, as those in the underground sought scapegoats for the frequent arrests of their comrades. Following the revolution, Stalin's enemies perpetuated these rumours and even forged documents to prove his guilt. But there is little evidence to support this theory, and most historians conclude that he spent more time in prison than one might expect if he had been working for the other side. Even Trotsky, in his biography of Stalin, concluded that 'it is unlikely that the accusers had definite proofs'.

When he was not engaged in daring escapes, Stalin spent his time in exile writing articles and corresponding with other revolutionaries, including Lenin, whose articles he had read as a seminarian in Tiflis, and whom he had met for the first time in Finland in 1905. In his periods of freedom, he frequently travelled abroad, spending time with Lenin in London in 1907 and representing the Bolshevik wing at several of the Party's Congresses. In 1912, he became part of the Bolshevik Central Committee. His mix of intellectual ability, tactical nous and ruthlessness had made Stalin indispensable to Lenin and the movement.

CHAPTER THREE

STALIN AND THE BOLSHEVIK TAKEOVER

Stalin spent the years leading up to 1917 in exile in a remote area of Siberia, isolated from the activities of Lenin and his Central Committee comrades. In his absence, the revolutionary struggle took a decisive turn. The outbreak of the First World War engendered a brief wave of patriotic support for the Tsar, which was soon extinguished as the realities of war set in. In February 1917, a riot in a bread queue snowballed into a full-scale insurrection, with workers on the streets demanding 'Peace, Bread and Land'. Tsar Nicholas II was forced to abdicate. Power was split between a Provisional Government made up of liberal

Stalin (left) and Lenin (right) in 1919

Duma deputies, which was to rule until a democratically elected Constituent Assembly could be convened, and the revolutionary Petrograd Soviet of Workers' and Soldiers' Deputies, a grassroots organ of direct democracy in which the Bolsheviks played a leading role.

Stalin arrived in Petrograd (as St Petersburg was then called) on 12th March 1917, and was there to meet Lenin at the Finland Station on his triumphal return from exile in Switzerland in April. Lenin immediately set out his plan to seize power in the name of the workers – a direct violation of Marxist doctrine – in a rhetorical *tour de force* known as the April Theses. Stalin, after a brief period of wavering, supported the Bolshevik leader, using the revolutionary newspaper *Pravda* to propagandise on behalf of the Leninist line. It is testament to his closeness to Lenin at this time that, when an attempt to seize power in July 1917 ended in failure, Stalin was the comrade chosen to hide Lenin in his flat, shaving off his beard and helping him flee to Finland.

In the events of October, however, it was Trotsky, not Stalin, who took centre stage. Trotsky (the revolutionary name of Lev Davidovich Bronstein) had sided with the Mensheviks in the Party split of 1903, and was regarded by the established Bolsheviks as something of an interloper. Trotsky was a gifted writer, orator and tactician, and he had played a leading role in the 1905 revolution, which gave him something of a rock-star status amongst revolutionaries. On his return to Russia from the United States in May 1917, he was reconciled with Lenin, formally joined the Bolshevik Central Committee and took charge of the Petrograd Soviet in September. He established a Military-Revolutionary Committee (pointedly not including Stalin) which quietly took control of the Petrograd Garrison and laid its plans for the armed seizure of power. In the early hours of 26th October, members of the MRC entered the Winter Palace, arrested the Provisional Government,

Lenin (left) and Trotsky during the October Revolution

and declared the foundation of a workers' state.

Stalin may have been 'behind the scenes' of the October Revolution, as Trotsky so dismissively put it, but he was certainly still in the heart of things. As troops seized the Winter Palace, he was with Lenin in the Bolshevik headquarters at the Smolnyi Institute in Petrograd, staying up around the clock writing, publishing decrees and preparing for power. He may not have been known to the wider public at this time, but he was trusted by the highest circles of the revolutionary movement. When the new government was proclaimed from the stage of the Congress of Soviets, 'I. V. Dzhugashvili-Stalin' was on the list as People's Commissar of Nationalities.

Having seized power, the Bolsheviks needed to cement it. They began by disbanding the Constituent Assembly, which had been democratically elected a month after the Bolshevik seizure of power, in November 1917, and in which the Bolsheviks were in the minority. With this act they 'declared war on that part of the country unwilling to accept Soviet power and the socialist revolution'.[7] Soon, the territory of the former Russian Empire was riven by civil war, which pitted the Reds (the Bolsheviks and their supporters) against the Whites (the opponents of Soviet power, ranging from supporters of the monarchy to Mensheviks and Socialist Revolutionaries), and the Greens (peasants who rose up against both Reds and Whites in defence of their villages and crops). Following the signing of a peace treaty with Germany at Brest Litovsk in March 1918, the Germans, the Allies and the Japanese joined the conflict in support of the Whites.

The Civil War was extraordinarily brutal, with numerous atrocities committed by all sides in support of their cause. The most high-profile casualties were Tsar Nicholas II and his family, gunned down in an Ekaterinburg basement by Bolshevik agents on 16th July 1918. Yet, as Laura Engelstein argues,

> in the end, the Bolsheviks proved the most adept at controlling and deploying violence, at shaping new instruments with which to impose social discipline and compel consent.[8]

They did so by means of the Red Army, a disciplined fighting force created by Trotsky and staffed by worker recruits and tsarist officers well-versed in military tactics (whose unsavoury class background was tolerated, if not accepted, for the defence of the revolution). This army conducted what became known as 'Red Terror' against the revolution's various enemies, including tsarist officials and the upper class, but often spilling over into ethnic pogroms and the slaughter of civilians.

Stalin was at the heart of this violent episode. Dispatched by Lenin to the city of Tsaritsyn on the Volga, 'his role, in essence, was Bolshevik bandit-in-chief in the south to feed the northern capital'.[9] Stalin worked to extract trainloads of grain from this fertile region by any means necessary, and to defend Tsaritsyn from attack. He took control of the local government and the regional branch of the Cheka (the newly created Bolshevik secret police, later known as the NKVD), and persuaded Trotsky to place him in charge of the local Red Army division of 20,000 men. He used these powers to uncover 'counter-revolutionary plots', conduct summary executions and propagandise on behalf of the socialist revolution. He was not fully successful; Tsaritsyn nearly fell to the

Whites in October 1918, and Trotsky persuaded Lenin to recall Stalin (although he would later deploy him again to the Urals, and to Lvov). These events, however, revealed much about him: his dedication to the cause, his willingness to use extreme violence to achieve his ends, and his distrust of the peasantry, who, he later explained, 'will not fight for socialism, will not! Voluntarily they will not fight.' All these traits would be amplified once he was in power.

Peter Holquist has referred to the period of violence and upheaval encompassing the First World War, the Russian Revolution, and the Civil War as Russia's 'continuum of crisis'. Estimates put the death toll at approximately 10 million, including those who died of famine and disease, the inevitable consequence of the Bolsheviks' harsh grain requisitioning policies. This 'continuum of crisis' transformed the revolutionary state and its future leader. The revolution was born of war and forged by war; the state it created was militaristic, hierarchical and supremely violent, even as it remained committed to the creation of an egalitarian, socialist utopia. These contradictions, embodied by Stalin, would be magnified as the Civil War gave way to an uneasy peace.

CHAPTER FOUR

THE PATH TO POWER

Stalin's transformation from Sukhanov's 'grey blur' to leader of the Communist Party (as the Bolshevik Party was renamed in 1919) was as meteoric as it was unexpected. Robert Service summarises the prevailing opinion in the 1920s that Stalin was 'a bureaucrat without an opinion or even personality of his own':

> His defects were thought obvious. Stalin had not lived
> as an émigré before the fall of the Imperial monarchy in
> the February Revolution! He was neither a polyglot nor a
> decent orator! He was a mere administrator! Such features
> were offered as proof that he deserved second-rate status
> among the party's leaders. [10]

By the end of the 1920s, however, Stalin had risen to prominence as 'first among equals' in the leadership of the Party and begun to cement his dictatorship. Historians have identified three main factors in this rise to power: his allegiance to Lenin, his abilities as a bureaucrat, and his talent for exploiting divisions amongst those around him.

Lenin died of a stroke in 1924, after shepherding the Party through revolution, a violent Civil War and the years of consolidation that followed. Stalin followed Lenin's lead during this time, lending his talents for organisation and bloodshed to the Civil War effort, but not distinguishing himself with any particular area of policy. Instead, he was content to act, in the words of Isaac Deutscher, as Sancho Panza to Lenin's Don Quixote. As Lenin's health declined, Stalin played the go-between for the revolutionary government and the ailing leader, who had retreated to his estate in Gorkii. Stalin derived much status from this position as Lenin's disciple and close personal friend. Following his death, Stalin moved quickly to cement his position as keeper of Lenin's memory and, by extension, his natural successor, organising his funeral, arranging for his embalmed body to be displayed in a mausoleum on Red Square, and beginning to give public lectures on Lenin's political thought (which, naturally, he best understood).

There were some problems in this self-presentation as Lenin's heir; not least that, in the last year of Lenin's life, the two had a violent quarrel that threatened Stalin's position in the Party. Following a political dispute, Stalin had been particularly rude to Lenin's wife, Nadezhda Krupskaia, over the telephone, a *faux pas* that Lenin took as a slight against himself. In late 1922, with an eye on the succession, Lenin dictated a document analysing the strengths and weaknesses of his Central Committee colleagues. This document, known as his 'Testament', contained some choice criticisms of Stalin:

> Com. Stalin … has concentrated immense power in his hands, and I am not sure whether he will always be capable of exercising that power with sufficient caution.[11]

He later commented that Stalin was 'too rude' to be in power. This document would have certainly caused Stalin much damage, had he not succeeded in suppressing it; the damning sentence was left out when the testament was read to the X Party Congress in 1921. It would be shockingly 'rediscovered' by Nikita Khrushchev in his Secret Speech denouncing Stalin in 1956.

Lenin's concern that Stalin had concentrated 'immense power' referred to his position in the Party bureaucracy, which he had been quietly consolidating since 1917. In 1922, Stalin had become General Secretary of the Central Committee, a seemingly menial role that involved monitoring personnel issues and setting the agenda for meetings of its governing Politburo. For his fellow revolutionaries, who concerned themselves with the big questions of ideology and government, such pencil-pushing tasks were beneath them: they mockingly referred to Stalin as 'Comrade Card-Index'. As General Secretary, however, Stalin was in a position to run – and indeed shape – the developing apparatus of government. His ability to recommend colleagues for promotion gave him immense power, and his efficiency gained him admirers and friends. As one colleague commented,

Now I have got to know him, I have extraordinary respect
for him... Under his stern demeanour is an attentiveness to
those he works with. We're creating order in the CC. [12]

By the late 1920s, the title of General Secretary had changed its
significance: no longer menial, it now denoted leadership.

Finally, Stalin's rise to the top was made possible by divisions
among the leadership. This discord centred on the figure of
Trotsky, whom Lenin had also criticised in his Testament for dis-
playing 'excessive self-assurance'. Stalin and Trotsky had a genuine
dislike of each other which had festered during the Civil War,
with Trotsky accusing Stalin of fomenting 'anarchy' in the regions,
and Stalin complaining to Lenin about Trotsky's 'unhinged com-
mands' and '"leftist" gesturing'. Many comrades were concerned
about Trotsky's pretensions to leadership; his role as head of the
Red Army in the Civil War gave him considerable practical power,
and his status as star revolutionary rivalled even Lenin's – so much
so that in 1921 Lenin moved to limit his influence by culling his
supporters in the bureaucracy.

When Lenin died, Trotsky attempted to rally support for a 'Left
Opposition' within the Party. It was a mistake. Stalin now had
new allies and, during the 1920s, he kept shifting his allegiance
amongst the seven members of the Politburo in order to isolate
Trotsky. A 'troika', consisting of Stalin, Lev Kamenev and Grigorii Zinoviev (acting Party Chairman during Lenin's illness),
succeeded in removing him from his position as People's Commissar of Military and Naval Affairs in 1925. The following year,
when Kamenev and Zinoviev shifted their support to Trotsky,
Stalin allied with Nikolai Bukharin and Alexei Rykov to oust

Trotsky from the Politburo.

Trotsky fought back, famously calling Stalin the 'gravedigger of the revolution'. But it was too late. By 1927, Trotsky, Zinoviev and Kamenev had all been expelled from the Party, accused of holding views that were incompatible with Party membership. Trotsky was exiled to Kazakhstan in 1928, and expelled from the USSR in 1929. He was murdered on Stalin's orders in Mexico in 1941.

In waging war against the 'Left Opposition' of Trotsky and his followers, and then subsequently against what he labelled as the 'right deviation' of Bukharin and others, Stalin slipped easily into a position of leadership. His talent for conspiracy and his ruthlessness in seeking out enemies, forged in the Caucasian underground, allowed him to move effectively against former colleagues. His war against Trotsky also allowed him to paint himself as a moderate Party man, a centrist whose allegiance to Lenin showed his reliability: next to Trotsky's melodramatic villain, Stalin was the paper-pusher whose reputation for efficiency gained him tremendous respect from his colleagues. In 1927, in a supreme act of political theatre, Stalin submitted his resignation as General Secretary: such a 'tough' man was no longer needed now the Opposition had been crushed. Needless to say, the Party refused to accept. Stalin's status as leader was assured.

CHAPTER FIVE

STALIN'S WOMEN

Accounts of Stalin's life tend to revolve around men. Unlike Lenin, who worked well with female revolutionaries, not least his wife, Nadezhda Krupskaia, Stalin's coterie was almost exclusively male. As Simon Sebag-Montefiore recounts:

> Women ranked low on his list of priorities, far below revolution, egotism, intellectual pursuits and hard-drinking dinners with friends.[13]

Women did play a significant role in Stalin's life, however, and one that seeped out from the domestic sphere to affect his political world. His relationships with his mother, wives, lovers and daughter permeate his life story and reinforce the impression we have of a mercurial man who was often passionate, but whose passions were tempered by a real desire for control.

Probably the most dominant woman in his life was his mother, Keke Dzhugashvili. Keke shaped young Stalin's life, instilling a love of learning and determination to succeed in the young boy. She pulled every string to get him a place in the Gori and Tiflis Seminaries, and to protect him from his father's malign influence. During his years of revolutionary activity, Keke continued to try to protect her son, sending him clothes and money for bribes to help him escape from Siberian exile.

Stalin's relationship with his mother was far from straightforward. She was a complicated woman, whose flirtatious nature attracted gossip but who could be harsh: by Stalin's own account, she 'beat [him] mercilessly' when he was a child. Following his rise to power, they rarely saw one another; Keke chose to remain in Georgia, living comfortably there until her death in 1935. Stalin was able to express real affection for her at this remove; later in life he would write to her tenderly:

How are you getting on, how are you feeling? I haven't had any letters from you in a long time: you must be upset with me, but what can I do? I'm really very busy. [14]

This affection-at-a-distance is significant. There is ample evidence that Stalin idealised and romanticised women, but was not entirely sure how to deal with them in real life. This can be seen in his (numerous) romantic entanglements, which have been carefully traced by Sebag-Montefiore. His flirtatious nature is evident: one

postcard to a girlfriend ends with

I owe you a kiss for the kiss, passed on to me by Peter. Let
me kiss you now. I'm not simply sending a kiss but am kissing you passionately (it's not worth kissing any other way).[15]

Romances with fellow revolutionaries, comrades in exile and passing acquaintances seem to have been carried out wholeheartedly,
but fleetingly: most he left without saying goodbye. This is particularly disturbing in the case of Lidia Pereprygina, a 14-year-old
with whom Stalin had a relationship while in exile in Kureika in
1914-16. Stalin was 34 at the time. There are rumours that she

Stalin's first wife, Ekaterina Svanidze (left), who died in 1907. He then married Nadezhda Allilueva
(right), until her death in 1932

had a child with him; after leaving Siberia, he never saw her again.

His relationship with both his wives seems to confirm this volatility. Stalin married his first wife, Ekaterina Svanidze, during his time in the Tiflis underground. Ekaterina was a dressmaker and not part of the revolutionary movement; nevertheless, she was arrested as an accomplice of the movement soon after the wedding and imprisoned for two months. The couple spent a good deal of time apart, as Stalin dedicated himself to revolution. They had a son, Yakov, in March 1907. Later that year, after the couple moved to Baku, Ekaterina fell seriously ill and died. Stalin was distraught, threatening suicide and throwing himself into the grave during the funeral. He did not return to Tiflis or see his son for the next ten years.

In stark contrast to the pretty Georgian dressmaker, his second wife, Nadezhda Allilu, was at the heart of the movement. Her father, Sergei Alliluev, had worked alongside Stalin in the Tiflis underground, and Stalin was a frequent visitor to the family home throughout Nadezhda's childhood. There are rumours that he had had an affair with her mother, Olga. It was in the Alliluevs' flat that he lived for the tumultuous months leading up to the 1917 revolution, there that he hid Lenin as he escaped into exile following the July Days, and there that he fell in love with the 16-year-old girl (Stalin was 39). They married in 1919.

Nadezhda strove to be the model of the ideal Soviet 'activist wife'. She had two children by Stalin: Vasilii, in 1921, and Svetlana, in 1926. She also spent a considerable amount of time engaged in study and Party activism, enrolling in the Industrial Academy in 1929. She was not always successful. In 1921, she was expelled from the party for being 'ballast with no interest in the life of the party whatsoever'; she was only restored to member-ship through Lenin's intervention. She clearly found the model of femininity promoted by the Soviet state difficult to live up to, writing to a friend:

> In our time it's not very easy since there are such an awful lot of new prejudices, and if you're not working, then of course you're a baba [a backward, peasant woman].[16]

Though it is clear that Stalin and Nadezhda loved one other, it was a strained marriage, not helped by the pressures of his developing political career. Stalin was away a lot, which made his young wife jealous. She was mentally fragile: mental illness ran in her family, affecting her mother and siblings as well as herself. In 1932, at a Kremlin dinner to celebrate the anniversary of the October Revo-lution, the couple argued publicly. Nadezhda returned to their flat alone and shot herself through the heart with a pistol, a present from her brother, Pavel.

Some have argued that Nadezhda committed suicide as an act of protest against her husband's political actions, citing the vio-lent repression during the collectivisation campaign of 1928-31. There is little evidence for this. Stalin's family lived an isolated and, in many ways, charmed life, spending time with the families of other Soviet leaders in the Kremlin complex and at their subur-ban dachas. Whatever the cause of her suicide, Stalin responded to it with deep grief, but also resentment and a sense of betrayal. He would later comment: 'She did a bad thing; she maimed me.' Cer-tainly, rumours were rife following her death; one of the Kremlin maids was arrested for saying that Stalin had killed her.

It seems that he saw his romantic relationships only in relation to himself. Sebag-Montefiore quotes a Georgian comrade: 'Wife, child, friend were only okay if they didn't hinder his work and saw things his way. You had to know Soso to understand his love.' [17] Most historians suggest that Nadezhda's suicide was a turning point. He continued to have affairs – one, indeed, with the wife of Nadezhda's brother, Pavel – but he became increasingly solitary. He never married again.

Even if the women in Stalin's life were a disappointment to him, his policies projected a vision of an ideal Soviet woman in the 1930s that would shape the lives of millions. Soviet social policy under Stalin moved away from the image of the independent female comrade promoted during the Revolution, advancing instead the 'dual role' of woman as industrial worker and heart of the family. Abortion, which had been legalised in 1920, was banned again in 1936. Soviet wives were expected to support their husbands by making the home clean and civilized, and exhorting them to work harder in the service of the Soviet state; to combine their careers in the factory and farm with their 'natural role' as mothers of the future Soviet generation; and to give grateful thanks to 'our friend, our teacher, the beloved leader of the world proletariat, Comrade Stalin!'

It is clear that Stalin was most comfortable in this fatherly role. His relationship with his daughter Svetlana was particularly close; he called her 'little sparrow' and played the role of her secretary, following her orders in their day-to-day life ('I order you to take me to the theatre with you'). Svetlana later recalled that: 'All the love father had was for me and he told me it was because I looked like his mother.' Again, however, his relationship with her centred on his own needs, and became more complicated as Svetlana grew up. He was furious at her teenage relationship with the older Soviet film-maker Aleksei Kappler, and had the man arrested for espionage. He refused to meet her husband, a former schoolmate. She would later divorce him and marry a man Stalin approved of; the union did not last long. Svetlana defected to the United States in 1967 and died there in 2011.

Pravda *was the official newspaper of the Communist Party. The paper's name in English means 'Truth'*

CHAPTER SIX

THE STALIN REVOLUTION

Those observing Stalin in the power struggles of the 1920s might be forgiven for assuming that, beyond personal animosities and a broad allegiance to minority national affairs, he had no particular personal ideology to guide his actions, choosing instead to follow Lenin's line or alter his opinions to suit the moment.

Trotsky went one further, suggesting that Stalin actively opposed revolutionary values, ushering in a 'Soviet Thermidor' that reversed the gains of the early 1920s and allowed a new bourgeoisie to entrench themselves. An analysis of Stalin's policies and actions, however, reveals a coherent vision of what the Soviet Union was, and how it should develop, that dramatically altered the Soviet state from the moment his power was consolidated. As Sarah Davies and James Harris have recently shown, analysing Stalin's archive allows us access to 'a distinctive vision of the world: Stalin's world'.[18]

Stalin had been a committed Marxist since the Tiflis seminary. His revolutionary teachers, particularly Lenin, had only confirmed him in this view. Marxism was a socio-economic theory; it held that human history was advancing inexorably along a line of development that would culminate in capitalism, the most advanced form of economic system. Capitalism was deeply unequal, however, and inevitably, the workers would come to resent their exploitation, rising up to overthrow their bosses and take power – and the means of production – into their own hands. This revolution would usher in a 'communist' system, defined by collective ownership of property and free, equal labour, which would represent the end of history as we know it.

The difficulty for Russian Marxists was that, in the early 1900s, Russia was considered economically 'backward' in comparison to its European neighbours. Predominantly peasant, it had only begun to industrialise in the 1880s. As a result, in Marxist terms, its nascent working class was not sufficiently conscious of its position to seize power. It was revolutionary, yes – February 1917 had proved that – but not in the way that Marx had envisaged. The solution to this dilemma appeared to lie in the internationalist nature of Marx's vision. As revolution swept through Europe (as the Bolsheviks believed it inevitably would), divisions between nations would disappear, and the working class of advanced capitalist countries such as Britain and Germany would come to Russia's aid, helping her to develop the necessary systems and technologies to build the workers' utopia. This was the argument put forward by Lenin in 1917, when he persuaded the Bolshevik party to seize power and declare the foundation of a workers' state, calling for the 'Proletariat of the World' to 'Unite!'

It was on this internationalist point that Stalin's political theory began to differ from that of his friend and mentor. While Stalin was committed to revolutionary internationalism, that commitment shifted focus as the years passed and no other countries succumbed to revolution. Far from coming to the aid of the revolutionary state, Western Europe challenged her on every front, sending troops to overthrow the Bolshevik Party during the Civil War, and threatening invasion in the 1927 war scare with Britain. In this light, Russia's economic 'backwardness' was a deep vulnerability that threatened the USSR's very survival. As Stalin would argue in 1931:

> Those who fall behind get beaten. But we do not want to be beaten. One feature of the history of old Russia was the continual beatings she suffered because of her backwardness. She was beaten by the Turkish beys. She was beaten by the Swedish feudal lords. She was beaten by the Polish and Lithuanian gentry. She was beaten by the Japanese barons. All beat her – because of her backwardness… Such is the law of the exploiters – to beat the backward and the weak… That is why we must no longer lag behind.[19]

To address this perceived backwardness, in 1924 Stalin and Bukharin had proposed a new vision, that of 'Socialism in One Country'. With no one coming to save the fledgling workers' state, it was down to the Party to develop the advanced economy and widespread political participation of the workers that Marx had envisioned. This did not mean abandoning the goal of ultimately spreading the revolution internationally; Stalin's policy in the borderlands still sought aggressively to expand Soviet territory (a goal he would ultimately achieve in the final months of World War II, as the Red Army pushed across Europe to Berlin). Yet even this goal necessitated the creation of a strong, socialist USSR. In 1928, Stalin began to put this vision into practice.

Building socialism in the USSR relied heavily on an alliance between the peasantry and the workers known as the *smychka*. Through this alliance, the peasantry would provide grain for the cities, allowing for the development of heavy industry and the working class. Industry, in turn, would provide goods and advanced machinery (such as tractors) to the countryside, making grain production more efficient and releasing more peasants from agricultural labour to travel to the cities and become industrial workers. This allegiance would be immortalised in the lasting symbol of the Soviet state, the hammer and sickle. By bringing these allies together, the Party would be able to 'master nature' and harness the raw materials of the Soviet state to build an advanced industry and working class.

The question of how this *smychka* would develop was a matter of intense debate throughout the 1920s. Following the chaos of the Civil War, which had prompted widespread unrest and fears of a counter-revolution, Lenin argued that peasants had to be encouraged to sell their grain by the provision of consumer goods, and in 1921, he convinced the Party to adopt a New Economic Policy, which reintroduced some private trade into the USSR. This reintroduction of limited capitalism was deeply controversial, but Lenin presented it to the Party as 'one step back, two steps forward' – a necessary breathing space to allow the economy to recover. Stalin

Gulag workers building the White Sea–Baltic Canal

supported this line until 1928, when he broke with its principal architect, Bukharin, and argued that only top-down administration and centralised control could achieve the 'Great Breakthrough' needed in the economy. On this basis, he proposed transforming the economy by force.

The Stalin Revolution, as it has now become known, envisaged the wholesale transformation of Russia, from a 'backward', peasant country to an advanced industrial power. In 1928, the state planning agency, Gosplan, drafted a centralised economic plan that set ambitious targets for the development of agriculture and industry. This 'five-year plan', set to run from 1928 to 1932, was an optimistic assertion of the power of centralised state planning, and the ability of the USSR to 'catch up and overtake' the advanced capitalist countries in economic terms.

The first draft of the plan envisioned a growth in coal production from 35 million tons in 1927-28 to 75 million tons in 1932-33; the second draft of the plan raised that target to 95-105 million tons. As Oleg Khlevniuk notes, these were 'insanely ambitious economic goals', the achievement of which would be deeply violent and chaotic, characterised by the casual violence and lack of regard for human life that had been Stalin's trademark in his Georgian underground days.[20] Yet Stalin would frame these changes as a utopian fulfilment of the revolution's promise:

We are advancing full steam ahead along the path of industrialization — to socialism, leaving behind the age-old 'Russian' backwardness. We are becoming a country of metal, a country of automobiles, a country of tractors. And when we have put the USSR on an automobile, and the muzhik on a tractor, let the worthy capitalists, who boast so much of their 'civilization', try to overtake us![21]

The Stalin Revolution proceeded on a number of 'fronts' (borrowing the military language of Civil War). The first of these tackled the problem of the peasantry. In 1928, thousands of loyal party activists flooded the countryside to 'collectivise' agriculture. They deliberately provoked 'class war', dividing peasant families into categories of rich ('kulak'), middle and poor peasant, and demanding from the former quotas of grain that were so high that they threatened future harvests. Those who did not comply were arrested and either summarily shot, expropriated or exiled to Gulag settlements in remote regions of the USSR such as Kazakhstan, in a process known as 'dekulakisation'. The remaining peasants were forced into large, often state-run, collective farms.

The process was violent, and it was violently resisted. Peasants (particularly women) slaughtered livestock and opposed collectivisation with force – so much so that in 1930 Stalin was forced to retreat, allowing peasants to leave collective farms, and publicly blaming the violent 'excesses' of collectivisation on local activists who had become 'dizzy with success' (a shrewd rewriting of history that airbrushed out his own complicity in the violence). Yet this was only a temporary reprieve; by 1940, 96.9% of all peasant households were back in collective farms and providing vast quantities of grain to the state.

Collectivisation was clear evidence of Stalin's distrust of the peasantry, a distrust which had been formed during his Civil War years in the Volga region – if not before. He viewed peasants as 'backward' and 'dark' people who, with their propensity to hoard grain, threatened the construction of a working-class society. For Stalin, therefore, grain requisitions were part of a necessary war against the peasantry as a group, even though he couched this war in the language of class struggle and the 'liquidation of the kulaks as a class'. Indeed, his decision to requisition vast quantities of grain to sell abroad to fund industry, even when the harvests were devastatingly low, showed a striking lack of concern for peasant lives. The resulting famines of 1931-33 would claimed the lives of between five and seven million people, hitting Ukraine and the North Caucasus (the USSR's biggest grain producing regions) disproportionately hard. Lev Kopelev, a Soviet writer and former activist, described his experiences of the Ukrainian famine, now known as the Holodomor:

I was convinced that I was accomplishing a great and necessary transformation of the countryside; that in the days
to come the people who lived there would be better off for
it; that their distress and suffering were a result of their
own ignorance and the machinations of a class enemy; that
those who sent me – and I myself – knew better than the
peasants how they should live, what they should sow, and
when they should plough. In the terrible spring of 1933, I
saw people dying from hunger. I saw women and children
with distended bellies, turning blue, still breathing but
with vacant, lifeless eyes.[22]

The violence of collectivisation had a devastating impact on Soviet
society. Yet the transformation of agriculture and the breaking of
peasant resistance enabled the industrial transformation of Stalin's Great Break to take place, funded by the grain requisitions
and staffed by the 23 million peasants who flooded into the cities
from the countryside between 1926 and 1939. The state inaugu-
rated huge building projects, such as the Dneprostroi hydroelectric
dam and the Turkestan-Siberian Railway; developed the means to
extract the Soviet Union's abundant raw materials, such as coal,
minerals and lumber, and established plants to turn those materials
into chemicals, steel and electricity; and began the mass production
of plant machinery, tractors, and cars. At first, before Soviet 'red
specialists' could be trained to guide this transformation, expertise
from the west, including America, had to be recruited.

While the speed and scope of the transformation was historic –
'what the industrialists of England and America had done over half
a century or more, the Soviet Communist Party tried to achieve in

a decade'[23] – it resulted in chaos, shortages, waste of raw materials, and immense strain on workers and the environment. Yet in 1931, when the first five-year plan was declared complete (a year ahead of schedule), these problems were not raised. Instead, Stalin presented the Great Breakthrough as a roaring success. As Khlevniuk explains, he 'did not cite a single actual figure but simply proclaimed that the emperor was indeed wearing clothes'.[24]

Alexei Stakhanov (right), the miner celebrated by Stalin, explains his work to a colleague in 1943

Five facts about Stalin

1. Before becoming a full-time revolutionary, Stalin worked as a weatherman at the Tiblisi Meteorological observatory.

2. In 1913, Adolf Hitler, Lev Trotsky, Joseph Tito, Sigmund Freud and Joseph Stalin all lived within a few miles of each other in central Vienna.

3. One of the most popular boys' names in the 1930s was Mels, which stood for Marx-Engels–Lenin–Stalin.

4. Stalin loved to eat traditional Georgian food. One of his personal chefs was Spiridon Putin – Vladimir Putin's grandfather.

5. Stalin was nominated twice for the Nobel Peace Prize, in 1945 and 1948. upset that he had not won, in 1949 he created his own prize, the International Stalin Prize for Strengthening Peace among Peoples.

CHAPTER SEVEN

STALINIST SOCIETY

The Stalin era was not only about the construction of a modern, industrial economy; it also envisaged the coming-into-being of a new society and a new people, steeped in the values of socialism and working enthusiastically to build the new world. In the words of Nikolai Bukharin, the socialist economic transformation would turn alienated labourers 'into persons, into collective creators and organisers, into people who worked on themselves, into conscious producers of their own "fate", into real architects of their own futures'.[25]

Yet in the chaos of the Stalin revolution, the definition of this 'New Soviet Person', and the means by which he or she was to be brought about, were often in flux, subject to the whims of Stalin's dictates and the shifting priorities and pressures of a society in construction. As Mark Edele has argued, Stalinist society was

> an unstable social formation made up of various, interdependent and overlapping, but often also mutually exclusive and contradictory, and – more confusingly – continuously changing entities.[26]

At its heart, Stalin's vision of society combined Marxist radicalism and a belief in the supremacy of the workers with a strong streak of pragmatism and control, tendencies which can be traced back to his experiences in the underground and the Civil War. While Stalin argued in 1930 that 'we need to raise up, promote the role of the working class', he thought nothing of twisting Lenin's words to support his policies, and made it clear in the early 1930s that much of the radical, egalitarian ideology of the revolutionary period – which he referred to as 'infantile' – had no place in the new, industrialised Soviet world. The Marxist formula 'from each according to his ability, to each according to his needs' was replaced by a system of tiered wages and bonuses. From 1935, a new class of 'hero' workers emerged, known as Stakhanovites, in honour of the Donbas miner Alexei Stakhanov who, in a feat of labour and endurance, overfulfilled his quota of coal by 14 times in one record-breaking (if carefully stage-managed) shift. As Stalin explained in 1935, such a feat was only possible under socialism:

> Things are different under the Soviet system. Here the working man is held in esteem. Here he works not for the exploiters, but for himself, for his class, for society. Here

the working man cannot feel neglected and alone. On the contrary, the man who works feels himself a free citizen of his country, a public figure, in a way. And if he works well and gives society his best, he is a hero of labour, and is covered with glory. Obviously, the Stakhanov movement could have arisen only under such conditions.[27]

Instead of the social equality of the 1920s, therefore, Stalinist society was determined by an elaborate and hierarchical system of punishments and rewards that mediated people's lives and access to power. Individuals were expected to transform themselves through heroic labour in the service of the state, an act that would bring with it a sense of purpose and collectivism that would bind Soviet citizens together. In Stalin's USSR, 'work was the instrument and measure of normality'.[28] Those who worked poorly, who were habitually late or changed jobs too often would get a reputation as a 'breakdown', and would be subject to legal punishment from 1932. Those who showed themselves to be heroic workers, however, gained opportunities and material rewards. The Stakhanovites, in particular, were feted and rewarded with flats and cars, caviar and champagne, the heart of a new, meritocratic middle class.

While these new relationships between state and people created the sense of a new, modern society in the making in Soviet cities, the reality of Stalin's increasing control could be seen most clearly in the countryside, which struggled to recover from the violence of collectivisation and famine. As Lynne Viola notes,

for reasons of sheer necessity, the state would largely give up on its revolutionary-missionary aspirations in the countryside, choosing, pragmatically and cynically, to exert its domination over the peasantry through the control of vital resources, most especially grain. [29]

The collective farm, far from an institution that promoted a socialist way of life (as had originally been envisaged), became an instrument of state control, policing peasant labour and fining shirkers – although the state did permit peasants to solve the perennial problem of food supply by granting them small plots of land in order to grow food for themselves and their families. While peasant heroes did exist in popular propaganda – such as Pasha Angelina, the founder of the first all-women brigade of tractor drivers – they were accorded much less prominence than their worker counterparts. Soviet identity, in accordance with Marxist doctrine, was the preserve of the rapidly expanding urban workforce.

This transformation of the Soviet state and society has been seen by some historians, such as Nicholas Timasheff, as evidence that Stalinism saw a 'great retreat' from revolutionary values to pre-revolutionary forms of culture and top-down social control. Certainly, the society that emerged in the mid-1930s did not look like a traditional Marxist utopia, shaped as it was by rigid hierarchies, violent coercion and the rediscovery of 'bourgeois' forms of culture, including the consumerist lifestyle of the newly promoted Stalinist elites. Indeed, Trotsky, in *The Revolution Betrayed*, would argue that Soviet society remained split between 'the privileged upper strata, and the more deprived lower depths', and thus could not be described as fully socialist.[30] For most modern historians, however, the changes brought about by Stalin represent another revolutionary moment, in which a 'new civilization' was being built, albeit by increasingly repressive means.

Indeed, Stalin's revolution had its own 'civilising mission', which sought to inculcate fresh ways of thinking and to develop the working-class 'consciousness' that Marx had envisaged through programmes of political activism and mass education, and the promotion of cultural values that reshaped the everyday lives and world view of Soviet subjects. Stalinist citizens were expected to be literate and informed, conversant with the works of Marx and Lenin, with developments in world affairs, and with the achievements of Soviet industry and culture. They were also pushed to acquire *kul'turnost*, or 'culturedness': a 'New Soviet Person' would be clean and well-dressed, eat politely at tables with white tablecloths, master a wide range of general and cultural knowledge, read widely, attend the theatre and cinema, grasp the complexities of Marxist dialectical materialism, and not swear.

New Soviet People were expected to talk about themselves in particular terms, as agents of history and constructors of a different world: to 'speak Bolshevik', in Stephen Kotkin's phrase.[31] They wrote diaries detailing their transformation into ideal Soviet citizens and produced appropriate autobiographies (akin to CVs) which detailed their class background and 'conversion' to Soviet consciousness. Many modern historians argue that these practices 'produced' a new kind of revolutionary identity, allowing a diverse range of Soviet citizens to embrace official ideology in the search of what Jochen Hellbeck has described as 'a purposeful and significant life':

Anyone who wrote himself into the revolutionary narrative

acquired a voice as an individual agent belonging to a larger whole. Moreover, in joining the movement individuals were encouraged to transform themselves. The power of the Communist appeal, which promised that those who had been slaves in the past could remold themselves into exemplary members of humanity, cannot be overestimated.[32]

So how was this attempt to define Soviet identity reconciled with the demands of ethnic minorities and other marginal groups? The question of how to deal with the diversity of the former Russian Empire had preoccupied tsarist and revolutionary leaders alike, and Stalin – particularly in his role as Commissar of Nationalities – played a key role in defining the central Bolshevik policy towards minority nationalities, known as *korenizatsiia*, or 'indigenisation'. This policy saw minority nationalities given their own territories, written scripts and folk culture, and minority representatives (with an appropriate class background, of course) appointed to key positions in government. In light of these policies, Terry Martin has referred to the Soviet Union as an 'Affirmative-Action Empire'. The only group without such ethnically defined institutions and cultural practices were the Russians – the result of Soviet fears of their 'great power chauvinism' – prompting Geoffrey Hosking to define Russians as the 'rulers and victims' of Soviet socialism.

Korenizatsiia was not the promotion of nationalism for its own sake, however – both Lenin and Stalin regarded nationalism as intrinsically dangerous. It was designed instead to cement Soviet power and build the revolution. The slogan of the policy was 'national in form, socialist in content': fixed national territories, arranged in an ethnically federal state, would enable formerly nomadic or dispersed ethnic groups to be served by socialist institutions; written scripts and folk culture would serve as conduits for Soviet propaganda; national sentiments would promote modernisation and class development. This tension between promoting and restricting national sentiments resulted in an uneasy coexistence of 'hard-line' and 'soft-line' policies to manage the Soviet nationalities.

The job of soft-line institutions was almost exclusively positive: to service, increase, and celebrate the number of national territories, schools, newspapers, theaters, written languages, museums, folk music ensembles, and so forth. The job of hard-line institutions was much more negative: to engage in surveillance over the implementation of nationalities policy and, when necessary, to take measures to prevent the intended development of national self-consciousness from evolving into an undesired growth of separatist nationalism.[33]

While some of the more radical, soft-line aspects of korenizatsiia were toned down in the 1930s, and the number of minority ethnicities granted their own territorial republics shrank dramatically, the idea that ethnic difference served as a means to bring people into the socialist community (as well as to mediate their access to power, and to police their ability to act in opposition to Soviet frameworks) persisted throughout the Stalin era. It would also inform the violent actions against minority nationalities during the Purges and World War II.

The same policy prevailed in dealing with other marginalised groups, such as the disabled, for whom socialism, understood in terms of labour, 'consciousness' and loyalty to Stalinist power, held out the promise of 'overcoming' their disabilities and becoming fully-fledged Soviet people, even as it limited and policed the conditions under which that transformation could be achieved.

The Stalin revolution had shaped a society that was both radical and traditional, utopian and coercive, egalitarian and deeply hierarchical, marked by difference and striving for homogeneity. It sought definitively to answer Marx's question of what socialism should look like. But while it provoked some critics to question whether it could be truly understood as socialist at all, this was a society that, above all, demanded an engagement with the ideology of socialism and a commitment to the figure of Stalin himself. As Stephen Kotkin has argued,

Stalinism was not just a political system, let alone the rule of an individual. It was a set of values, a social identity, a way of life.[34]

CHAPTER EIGHT

THE STALIN CULT

S talin's 'cult of personality' was first openly discussed by Nikita Khrushchev in 1956, during his so-called 'Secret Speech' to the XX Party Congress, a speech which revealed the former leader's crimes both to the Russian people and to the world. The use of the word 'cult' was certainly meant to be derogatory. For Khrushchev, the violent excesses and abuses of power of the Stalin era could only be attributed to his desire for personal glory and inability to tolerate those who thought differently to himself.

Comrades, the cult of personality acquired such monstrous size chiefly because Stalin himself, using all conceivable methods, supported the glorification of his own person. [35]

Such glorifying of one man, in the context of a nominally 'equal' society, seems to confirm our worst fears about Stalin – his self-aggrandisement, his psychopathy, his self-centredness – and remind us of the brainwashing of those he ruled. The glorification of his persona puts him in the same universe as Hitler, Mussolini, Mao Tse-tung, and Kim Jong-Il. Recent studies of Stalin's personality cult, however, have shown it to be more complex than previously thought, and to have been carefully fostered by modern political techniques.

The historian Jan Plamper has traced how, after the revolution, Bolshevik leaders began casting about for heroes to venerate. As early as 1919, Lenin was making plans to build statues honouring fathers of the Left, including Marx and Engels. Following his death, the embalming of his body gave Lenin himself the status of living saint. The glorification of Stalin began in the same vein in 1929, with a special edition of *Pravda* on the occasion of his fiftieth birthday.

By the mid-1930s, the Stalin cult encompassed oil paintings, posters, biographies, children's books, and the renaming of streets, and cities. Some 1930s films included scenes in which the heroes travelled to Moscow to see Stalin (who would appear through spliced-in documentary footage, or played by the actor Mikheil Gelovani). Poetry and song glorified the great leader, and Soviet children were encouraged to say 'Thank you Comrade Stalin!' for their happy childhoods. As one popular 'Song of Stalin' concluded:

Sunny prospects are open before us
The flames of victory blaze over the country

Comrade Stalin lives for our happiness
Our wise leader, our dear teacher.

Stalin publicly resisted his veneration, painting himself as a modest man and a faithful disciple of Lenin. However, it would have been difficult for a cult such as this to be created against his will. For Plamper, this 'immodest modesty' was as much a part of the cult as the overblown glorification that accompanied it, and demonstrates the role Stalin played in orchestrating his own public persona.[36] In the 1990s, archival drafts of Stalin's 1947 biography were released, which showed that Stalin had inserted the following:

Masterfully performing the job of *vozhd* of the party and people and enjoying the full support of the Soviet people, Stalin nevertheless did not allow even a shadow of self-importance, conceit, or self-admiration into anything he did.[37]

It is clear that he was intimately involved in the promotion – and censorship – of material about his own image, choosing what to release and what to suppress. In the publication of his writings, he was vigilant, annotating drafts and controlling how they were translated. The image conveyed was of a glorious but benevolent man, whose care for his subjects was boundless, and whose every effort was directed towards the betterment of their lives and the country.

In person, of course, he was vastly more complicated and mercurial, especially after the death of his second wife, Nadezhda. On the one hand, Sebag-Montefiore describes him as 'what is known now as a "people person"'; he was warm and genial, and went out of his way to charm people. He liked to tease and play practical jokes. His friendships were intense and playful. While in exile in 1912, he wrote to Kamenev: 'Greetings friend! I rub your nose in an Eskimo kiss. Dammit. I miss the hell out of you.' He would hold raucous, drunken dinners at his dacha and sing choral trios with Voroshilov and Mikoyan. He was also a careful and meticulous colleague, preparing diligently for meetings and impressing underlings with his care and consideration. Yet at the same time, he could be cruel and vindictive. Oleg Khlevniuk writes:

> At some point in their careers, virtually everyone in the top Soviet leadership had to endure a ritual of humiliation and repentance followed by renewed oaths of allegiance to the *vozhd*.[38]

In these moments, his temper was explosive and his language was foul, sending loyal comrades running for cover. Stalin was not simply hot-headed; he also held grudges. As the Purges took hold, not only those who had wronged him, but his closest friends frequently found themselves accused of horrific crimes against the state. This included Kamenev, for whom the promise of Eskimo kisses and eternal friendship made way for a show trial and summary execution. The cult thus represented a careful retelling of Stalin's personal attributes, and a smoothing over of his problematic and vindictive personality. Indeed, he was fully aware of the gap between his own personality and his cult portrayal. As he once explained to his son, Vasilii:

COUNTING THE DEAD

Stalin's political career coincided with – and in many cases, caused – one of the bloodiest periods in human history. From recently declassified files, we know that, during the year and a half of the Great Purge, 1.6 million people were arrested and 700,000 shot. This equates to 1,500 killed per day. Those who escaped execution were imprisoned in a system of 'rehabilitative' labour camps known as the Gulag, in the most inhospitable areas of European Russia, Siberia and Central Asia. Conditions were so bad that thousands died – 90,564 in 1938 alone.

Soviet death rates are not without controversy. The Soviet state kept meticulous records, but historians still remain sceptical; as Alec Nove has explained, pressures on those doing the recording to downplay issues of famine, misrepresent causes of death or to over exaggerate population movement and exile makes it difficult to trust these numbers. Estimates of casualties during the 1930s range from 600,000 to 20 million. Robert Conquest insists that "the total of

deaths caused by the whole range of the Soviet regime's terrors can hardly be lower than some thirteen to fifteen millions".

The figures for Purge deaths must also be seen in the context of the long view of the early 20th century. Violence and mass death during this period came in successive waves. Peter Holquist refers to Russia's "continuum of crisis", a period of upheaval encompassing the First World War, the Russian Revolution, and the Civil War. Estimates here put the death toll at approximately 10 million, including those who died of famine and disease. Deaths during collectivisation and industrialisation are thought to number around seven million, including the five million who died during the Ukrainian famine of 1932 known as the "Holodomor". The Purges themselves only wound down shortly before the outbreak of the Second World War, during which 27 million Soviet citizens died. The demographic impact of these mass casualties – which, as is always the case with war, disproportionately affected men – is still being felt.

Mass graves were built, and quickly filled, during the Purges

You're not Stalin and I'm not Stalin. Stalin *is* Soviet power. Stalin is what he is in the newspapers and the portraits, not you, not even me![39]

The question, of course, is why? Historians have put forward a variety of explanations for the cult of personality (leaving aside the assumption that Stalin created it for his own nefarious purposes). For Roy Medvedev, the cult was in some ways inevitable, as the Revolution 'brought such sweeping changes in such a short time that the leaders seemed to be miracle makers'.[40] For Jeffrey Brooks, the celebration of Stalin served a practical purpose, creating a sort of contract with the populace, in which no effort would be enough to repay the beloved leader for his benevolent care. This 'moral economy', he argues, was necessary to ensure loyalty and participation in a time of vast social change. David Brandenberger has argued that the personality cults of Lenin and Stalin were necessary to unite a diverse society that had little else in common, and to make abstract Marxist theories accessible to the masses. For Plamper, the Stalin cult was a product of 'alchemy', a transformative process that took these disparate impulses and turned them into something with far greater meaning.

The Stalin cult is also cited as evidence that Russians inevitably gravitate towards a certain kind of leader; a 'strong hand' who, like Putin, can defend Russia from outside threat and project an image of masculine decisiveness. It is clear that Stalin was aware of this idea, drawing explicit parallels between himself and other 'strong leaders' such as Aleksandr Nevskii and Ivan the Terrible.

Personality cults were not simply confined to the leader, however. The celebration of individual heroes, such as the hero worker

Aleksei Stakhanov, was a central part of Stalin-era culture. The disabled author Nikolai Ostrovskii, who 'overcame' his physical infirmities to write a prize-winning novel, *How the Steel was Tempered*, was widely celebrated. These lesser cults served to reinforce Stalin's own, offering their own gratitude and service to the *vozhd*.

The Stalin cult reveals another important aspect of Stalinist culture. Celebrations of Stalin fed into a broader 'celebration discourse', as Karen Petrone terms it, including parades, mass meetings and family parties, which shaped everyday life in the 1930s. Stalin had announced in 1935 that 'Life has become better, comrades: Life has become more joyous'. In response, Soviet citizens gathered together to celebrate the successes of the Soviet regime and to experience the prosperity that the 'Great Breakthrough' had brought. During times of terror, the symbols of the Soviet state – including Stalin – represented a key tool in fostering social unity and allowing individuals to feel part of a society that, in other circumstances, might have fractured under the strain.

The Stalin Cult was promoted through a wide variety of media. Portraits and statues of the great leader adorned public buildings and city squares. Millions of copies of Stalin's collected works were published in all languages. He also lent his name to many things. A commemorative volume published in honour of his seventieth birthday, in 1949, contains a pull-out entitled 'In the Name of Stalin', filled with photographs of forty-two institutions bearing the name of the *vozhd*: the Stalin Moscow Car Factory, the town of Stalinogorsk, the leisure steamer 'Joseph Stalin', the 'Stalinets' tractor, as well as numerous Stalin collective farms, Stalin squares and Stalin universities.

He also oversaw many grandiose building projects, a surprisingly large number of which still endure. The Moscow Metro, which bore the name of his colleague Lazar Kaganovich, was completed under his leadership; he and his children, Svetlana and Vasilii, took an impromptu ride in 1935. A set of imposing gothic sky-scrapers surrounding Moscow, built after the Second World War, are known as the Stalin Towers (or in English, the Seven Sisters). During the Stalin Plan of 1936, Moscow's roads were widened, 'monumental buildings' were constructed and the city acquired a green belt and a network of parks. Somewhat less practical was his plan to build a series of canals to link Moscow to the major rivers of Russia, thus making the city 'a port to five seas'. The Stalin White Sea-Belomor Canal was completed using forced labour in 1934; the Moscow-Volga canal opened in 1937. No sooner were these waterways opened, however, than they were found to be too shallow to accommodate ships. The most grandiose (and unful-filled) of these projects was for a Palace of the Soviets, to be built on the site of the Cathedral of Christ the Saviour in Moscow. The building was to be the tallest in the world, eight metres above the Empire State Building, and topped with a 90-metre statue of Lenin, his head, appropriately enough, in the clouds.

Following Stalin's death, these projects and objects had an uneasy afterlife. During de-Stalinization, portraits and books were easy to pulp, but statues had a permanency that made their destruction hard; a number of them can still be found in Moscow's Fallen Monuments Park. Those cities and institutions named for Stalin were hastily renamed. Yet the old names still linger. Volgo-grad residents have petitioned to restore the name of Stalingrad to their city, in honour of the victorious battle of Stalingrad during the Second World War, and the city bears the name of Stalingrad every year on Victory Day. In 2009, the refurbishment of the Kurskaya metro station controversially reinstated the inscription: 'Stalin raised us on loyalty to the people and inspired us to labour and great feats.'

The Red Army theatre in Moscow, built in the shape of the Red Star

CHAPTER NINE

THE LIMITS OF STALIN'S POWER

On 5th December 1936, the Soviet government ratified a new constitution, known informally as the Stalin Constitution. The Constitution set out an ambitious and positive vision for a society under construction, acknowledging the achievements that had been made during the period of collectivisation and industrialisation, and establishing the fundamental rights and freedoms to be enjoyed by all Soviet citizens. The new constitution was widely celebrated; as the newspaper *Izvestiia* announced, Soviet citizens should 'celebrate and be proud!' of the Stalin Constitution, which was 'an historic document, towering over the history of the world like a giant beacon, lighting the way for all mankind'.

As the overblown rhetoric suggests, the Stalin Constitution was a carefully staged piece of propaganda, setting out the achievements of the USSR to both domestic and international audiences. The Constitution was seen to mark a turning point in Soviet history, as society moved from the upheaval of the Great Breakthrough to a period of social and political consolidation. It signalled a shifting of priorities; a move away from the 'class war' that had character-ised the post-revolutionary period towards a new, equal, socialist way of life. Strikingly, the Stalin Constitution promised the right to vote to all citizens over the age of eighteen, regardless of their class background, alongside universal civil liberties including free-dom of speech and conscience, the right to work and the right to leisure.

The Constitution raises important questions about the shape of Stalinist society and the limits of his power. Histories of Stalinism that emerged in the West following his death – products of the early Cold War – described his period of rule as 'totalitarian', com-paring it directly to Nazi Germany and arguing that, under his leadership, the state achieved total control over society, and Stalin total control over the state. This 'totalitarian thesis', problematic though it is, has proved particularly difficult to shake. One recent history of the Stalin period begins: 'No person in history had such a direct impact on the lives of so many as Joseph Stalin had during his lifetime.'[41] The direct line from the mind of Stalin to the lives of millions is clearly understood.

The Stalin Constitution complicates this picture, both in its rhetoric of freedom and democracy, and in the practices that surrounded its creation. The Constitution was a major public undertaking: drafted by a series of committees and sub-commit-tees under Stalin's direction, it was submitted to the public for widespread consultation on 12th June 1936. Over the course of six months, 623,224 public meetings were held, attended by 42 million people, who then submitted 169,739 proposals, additions and amendments, which were periodically published in the local and central press. The publication of the draft was celebrated with a carnival in Gorky Park, where revellers in fancy dress danced until the small hours.

Public response to the draft Constitution was mixed; while many respondents followed the usual formula of thanking Comrade Stalin for their happy lives, others voiced more critical opinions.[42] Some viewed the entire exercise as misguided, especially as the negative impact of industrialisation were still being felt: 'We don't need your Constitution, we need bread and cheap food.' Others felt that talk of fundamental freedoms was impossible with the secret police (NKVD) still in existence. But many actively debated the substance of the various clauses, with many defending what they understood as 'Soviet values' against the state. There was considerable public opposition, for example, to the clause that allowed religious believers to stand for public office, which was seen as a direct challenge to the official atheism of the Soviet state.

The debates surrounding the Stalin Constitution have been described by Geoffrey Hosking as the 'first germ of Civil Society' [43] in the Soviet period. This is a questionable assertion; while these meetings enabled Soviet citizens to discuss the shape of their country publicly, and give voice to their opinions on personal and state matters, there were clear limits to the debate. Moreover, the Constitution raised expectations of political consolidation and democracy that were at odds with the arbitrary violence and repression of the Stalinist state – expectations which remained after the Constitution's ratification. It thus raised important questions about the rights of Soviet citizens: 'it is not insignificant that over succeeding decades most protests against the arbitrariness of political power began by invoking the fundamental laws of the constitution'.[44] Serhy Yekelchyk notes that

> while demonstrating their allegiance to the state in many formulaic ways, Stalinist citizens also found within the rigid political rituals a number of subtle ways to negotiate with, question, mock, and resist the state apparatus.[45]

As these historians suggest, it is difficult to see Stalin's power as absolute. Certainly, aspects of his rule can be identified as 'totalising' in their impulses. In Stalin's push to build 'socialism in one country', he attempted to develop a set of plans and policies that would bring all aspects of everyday life – from grain production to personal hygiene – under the guidance of the Party. Coercion was frequently used to ensure compliance.

But these efforts were hardly unique to Stalin, mirroring broader European impulses to 'civilise' the lower classes and deploy expert intervention to improve people's lives (the founding principle, indeed, of the modern welfare state). David Hoffmann points out how patchy and incomplete these efforts were:

> the Soviet system failed to refashion all people in all ways. Most citizens, even as they inhabited a world of Soviet norms and values, continued to hold their own beliefs and pursue their own interests.[46]

How, then, might we understand the extent, and the limits, of

Stalin's power? According to Khlevniuk,

> Stalin kept himself at the centre of the huge machine used to manipulate officials. He initiated and guided repression, orchestrated all major reassignments, and was constantly reshuffling people so that nobody grew too comfortable in a particular job. Like any dictator, he strove to instil a sense of fear, adoration, and instinctive devotion in his underlings.[47]

Yet Stalin's political vision was also constrained by the bureaucracy of the Soviet party state. Despite his widely publicised ability to work tirelessly on the business of government, it was simply not possible for him to take every decision. He needed to delegate. In many ways, the bureaucracy was of his own making; his work in the 1920s had developed a set of hierarchies and chains of command that ensured the everyday functioning of the government. Yet he could not subvert these structures. During the Purges of 1937, for example, when, according to Party tradition, the Politburo was asked to vote on the arrests of military and party leaders: it is impossible to say what drove these men to write 'for' on the arrest lists, but the fact that they were required to do so is still significant.

Stalin's power was also limited by the public façade of collective leadership. As Khlevniuk has shown, 'periodic manifestations of oligarchy inevitably threatened Stalin's sole power'.[48] However scared they may have been of him, particularly as time went on and he became more angry and paranoid, his fellow leaders still had their own autonomy and ability to make administrative decisions. These personal power-bases were never permitted to grow too large, or to threaten Stalin's position. Yet he was still obliged to work within the system and find ways to promote his agenda. His 'team' was a key factor in his leadership:

> unchallenged top dog though he was, Stalin preferred – as his contemporaries Mussolini and Hitler did not – to operate with a group of powerful figures around him, loyal to him personally but also operating as a team.[49]

This team included such figures as Vyacheslav Molotov, chief negotiator of the Nazi-Soviet Pact; Lazar Kaganovich, Central Committee secretary and head of the Ukrianian and Moscow parties; Anastas Mikoyan, Minister of Trade, and later of Food; and Kliment Voroshilov, Defence Minister until World War II.

One of the most significant pieces of evidence that Stalin did not have absolute power was his need to resort to modern techniques of persuasion – terror and mass enthusiasm – to achieve his ideological goals. It was certainly not the case that he could give orders and see them unthinkingly obeyed: he needed to bring the Party, and the people, with him. The transformation of Soviet industry and agriculture could not have taken place through top-down orders alone; it required the individuals involved to understand the broader significance of their labour – the building of a better world – and to drive themselves and their comrades to break every record and storm every fortress. Sharing, as one Stalinist subject wrote, the 'interests, hopes and dreams of the USSR' allowed individuals to become part of the broader process of putting Stalin's plans into action.[50]

When the limits of mass enthusiasm were reached, violence and coercion were used. They were two sides of the same coin; many of those most enthusiastic about the building of a utopian Soviet society were also those most convinced that violence was a necessary step to get there. Peter Holquist has suggested that the 'Bolshevik aspiration to cultivate a socialist society, and as part of that, to cultivate each individual, envisioned violence'.[51] Cutting out the unwanted portions of society, and forcing the rest to conform, was seen as essential in creating a new world. Yet the need to threaten, beat and kill is proof, if any were needed, that Stalin's orders themselves were not enough.

If the Soviet regime was not simply the plaything of a paranoid dictator, then what was it? Other, more complex, metaphors have been used to describe the functioning of the Party in this period. Katerina Clark, discussing culture, has spoken of an 'ecosystem'. Answering the 'old Leninist maxim "Who whom?"', she suggests that ideas and influences in the Stalinist period were not simply impositions, but formed in dialogue with practitioners of culture.[52] Stephen Kotkin, drawing on the work of Michel Foucault, has described Stalinism as a 'civilization', arguing that state policies and programmes

> formed part of the lives of people, ordinary and higher-ups alike, and their actions and reactions, initiatives and responses, in significant ways influenced how these programs were carried out, circumvented, and changed in unforeseen ways. [53]

There were other, practical constraints on Stalinist policies that were not unique to Soviet socialism. Like other leaders of modern states, Stalin needed to supply his people with food and fuel, maintain a functioning and efficient economy, deal with difficult terrain and inclement weather, and grapple with all sorts of different beliefs and prejudices (such as xenophobia, or religious faith) which conflicted with the Soviet world view. Kate Brown has suggested that when such pressures and priorities are taken into account, it is possible to argue that 'Kazakhstan and Montana [in the US] are nearly the same place' – by which she means that practical imperatives are often just as important as ideology in determining how power operates.[54] Moreover, the vast distances between Stalin's seat in the Kremlin and the Soviet Union's far-flung regions meant that policies were often decisively shaped by ad hoc decision making on the ground, and bore little resemblance to the grand plans issuing from the top.

Of course it is true that Stalin was hugely decisively influential in shaping the historical period named after him. The personal factor was a significant part of the Stalinist story. Yet to reduce any phase of any country's history to the personality of its then ruler is to erase the complexities of life, and to ignore the processes by which social transformations, both benign and supremely violent, can develop. As Martin Malia concluded, 'Stalin was a bad man… but much more than this is needed to explain the momentous policies of his twenty-five year reign'. [55]

CHAPTER TEN

STALIN AT LEISURE

Even at the height of the Great Breakthrough, Stalin did not spend all his time on the business of state. He was certainly a driven leader and his daily routine was punishing; he rose at 11, took lunch at 4, dinner at 9 and worked well into the small hours, insisting that his subordinates do the same. Yet he did have a varied set of interests that give some insight into the inner life of the *vozhd*, whose tastes and habits shaped expectations for party colleagues and ordinary Soviet citizens alike.

Stalin's ability to read was legendary. He boasted that he read up to 500 pages per day. These included great volumes of state papers, including reports from state institutions, foreign and military ministries and intelligence bodies, but also magazines, books and newspapers. He was a fan of history, seeking out anything to do with Peter the Great and Ivan the Terrible, whom he saw as models for his style of leadership. He also read novels; among the 20,000 books in his library, his favourites were the works of Gogol, Chekhov, Thackeray and Balzac. This compulsion to read is perhaps unsurprising for a revolutionary of his generation; like most of his comrades, he had developed extensive reading habits while in exile. Stalinist citizens were also expected to emulate this habit and achieve a wide and varied knowledge of and understanding of the world through reading socialist-realist and classical literature as well as ideological tracts.

Stalin was also an obsessive film buff. The state-of-the-art cinema in the Kremlin was frequently used for screenings of classics – both Western and Soviet – and new films in development. The cinema was a site of diplomacy: Stalin would take members of the Politburo and his foreign guests, such as Marshal Tito, to watch films and ask for their opinions. But it was also a site of pleasure. Stalin was a particular fan of Charlie Chaplin, and, during World War II, he acquired Goebbels's film collection. According to Sebag-Montefiore, he particularly enjoyed detective films and westerns, but could not abide titillation. His favourite film was Grigorii Aleksandrov's *Volga Volga*, a musical comedy about an amateur music troupe trying to make it to Moscow to perform in the Moscow Musical Olympiad. It is perhaps ironic that Stalin's favourite film was a comedy that poked fun at representatives of Soviet power: the villain of the piece, Byvalov, is a careerist and petty bureaucrat whose ambitions are thwarted by the young members of a provincial theatre group. Stalin had seen the film so many times that he knew the script by heart, and would recite each line just before the actor.

He was not just a consumer of culture; he was also an active – if inconsistent – participant in its production. He involved himself in the careers of contemporary writers, such as Maksim Gorkii, Mikhail Sholokhov and Aleksei Tolstoi. He read drafts of novels, plays and screenplays, writing notes in the margins and giving the authors advice. He supervised movie scripts and rewrote dialogues and song lyrics. For Stalin, culture was not simply a source of pleasure, but a key tool in the transformation of society. Socialist realism, the cultural doctrine of his era, insisted on the depiction of 'reality in its revolutionary development': an idealised version of reality that would spur Soviet citizens on to great feats in the service of social transformation. For him, ideological purity, simplicity and accessibility were the watchwords of cultural success; he particularly criticised slow scenes in Soviet films for failing to show the 'new fast pace of life in the USSR'.[56]

While it would be a mistake to reduce the complex and contested cultural scene of the 1930s to the agency of one individual, Stalin's influence in cultural matters was significant. His role as the ultimate censor was such that films could not be released without his say-so; backlogs would mount up when he was on holiday on the Black Sea coast. He also had the power to make or break the artists themselves. In 1936, his negative reaction to Shostakovich's opera *Lady Macbeth of Mtsensk* led to the composer's formal denunciation on the pages of *Pravda* and his marginalisation in the music world. Many artists and writers perished in the Purges, including Isaac Babel and Vsevolod Meierkhol'd. The writer Mikhail Bulgakov was kept in a tortuous limbo for years, prevented from publishing or staging his plays, but forbidden to leave the country. For those Stalin liked, however, patronage and prestige (and some uncomfortable scrutiny) beckoned.

Stalin was also a prolific writer. Alongside the orders and decrees of state, he expounded his ideological world view in numerous speeches and articles in *Pravda*. As Oleg Khlevniuk notes, in his writings, Stalin 'strove for a clarity and conciseness that bordered on oversimplification',[57] a trait that the writer Isaac Babel would fulsomely praise at the All-Union Congress of Soviet Writers in 1934: 'just look at the way Stalin forges his speech, how chiselled his spare words are, how full of muscular strength'.[58] Stalin's writing had not always been so functional, however. He had begun writing in his native Georgian as a child, and at the age of 15, he published the poem 'Morning':

The rose's bud had blossomed out
Reaching out to touch the violet
The lily was waking up
And bending its head in the breeze.

High in the clouds, the lark
Was singing a chirruping hymn
While the joyful nightingale
With a gentle voice was saying:

'Be full of bloom, o lovely land,
Rejoice, Iberian's country,
And you, o Georgian, by studying
Bring joy to your motherland'[59]

This verse so impressed Ilia Ch'avch'avadze, the prominent writer and editor of the daily newspaper Iveria, that five of Stalin's poems were published over the course of 1895. As Donald Rayfield explains, the poem blends Persian, Byzantine and Romantic imagery with a Russian-style exhortation to the reader.[60] It also hints at some of the preoccupations – such as auto-didacticism and nationalism – that would inform many of his later policies.

While Stalin's position in Russian history is constantly being reassessed, his poetry endures. Published (without attribution) in Georgian school primers even during the height of Khrushchev's de-Stalinization campaign, his poetry is still being used by schoolchildren as they learn to read. New translations into English were produced in 2013. The incongruity of Stalin the poet complicates our understanding of him as a monster of history. Donald Rayfield writes:

> While it is true that a capacity for impromptu versification to pre-set formulas has long been normal among the Georgians, Stalin's efforts have an individuality and a response to Russian and Georgian traditions which show him to be less of a barbarian than his victims preferred to think.[61]

In the melee of revolution, Stalin abandoned his literary writings in favour of tracts on nationalism and socialist governance. In later life, he would turn his attentions to the field of science, and, in his attempt to 'live up to the ideal of a man who united political power and intellectual acumen', he 'intervened in scientific debates in fields ranging from philosophy to physics'.[62]

These interventions show him to be a man who understood the

world to be fundamentally shaped by scientific laws, and who believed that understanding these laws clearly would allow Soviet citizens to master nature and achieve modernity. He was wrong about a good deal, says Ethan Pollock. But 'we do not have to accept the intellectual value of Stalin's proclamations about biology, linguistics, physiology, or political economy to recognise that he consistently spent time on the detail of scholarly disputes'.[63]

Stalin's engagement with films, literature and popular science reveal his understanding of the value of these media as a tool in the furtherance of his political agenda; a means to shape the minds of the Soviet masses. His garden, however, was for himself alone. Historians have noted his love of roses and mimosas, his passion for growing lemon trees and pottering in the gardens of his succession of dachas near Moscow and holiday homes on the Black Sea. Intimate photographs taken after Nadezhda's death show him weeding unselfconsciously in the garden. While the symbolic parallels with his political role can be (and have been) made – Miriam Dobson writes that 'Stalinist gardening techniques included not only nurturing but also the destruction of anything that might damage the health of the nursery'[64] – Stalin's quiet moments in the garden seem a vast distance from the horrors of his rule.

CHAPTER ELEVEN

UNDERSTANDING THE PURGES

In the late 1930s, Soviet society was caught up in a wave of violent state repression known as the Purges. Following the 1934 murder of Stalin's close associate, the Leningrad Party boss Sergei Kirov, a series of elaborately staged show trials revealed treason at the heart of the Party, with Stalin's former colleagues Zinoviev, Kamenev, Piatakov, Radek, Bukharin and Rykov pleading guilty in open court to plots against the Soviet state. Following these trials, the secret police (the People's Commissariat of Internal Affairs, or NKVD) were tasked with searching for and removing from society spies, saboteurs and oppositionists who were trying to corrupt the Soviet system from within.

This hyper-vigilance and paranoia soon expanded out from

the political elites to encompass wider society. In July 1937, the NKVD promulgated its notorious 'Order No.00447', which instigated mass repressions against 'former kulaks, bandits, and other anti-Soviet elements'; these were followed by distinct 'operations' against kulaks and national minorities. By the time mass repressions wound down in the autumn of 1938, millions had been arrested and found guilty of being 'enemies of the people', then either shot immediately or imprisoned in the vast network of labour camps known as the Gulag.

Archival evidence has proved Stalin's intimate involvement in both the policy and the bureaucracy of the Purges. In speeches and articles in *Pravda*, he set out his belief in the existence of traitors and foreign spies in the Party and wider society. With his usual meticulousness, he ordered arrests and executions, took decisions over punishments, and read (and edited) transcripts of tortured confessions. In a perverse echo of his centralised economic planning, Order No.00447 set precise targets for arrests and executions that the NKVD took pains to overfulfil. Yet his personal emotions were also a powerful factor; many of those who lost their lives during the Purges were those who had wronged him at earlier moments in his career, such as his opponents in the power-struggles of the 1930s, or the relatives of his former wives. As Ronald Suny writes, Stalin and his lieutenants

shared a mentality that divided the world into enemies and friends and justified the harshest of measures against all opponents.[65]

While no one now disputes that Stalin was the instigator of this wave of repression, there remains serious debate amongst historians over his motives, and the reasons why the Purges were carried out. For many, they stand as evidence that, by the late 1930s, Stalin was suffering from a mental illness: eyewitnesses commented on his 'mad fits of rage' and lack of control. Others point to more strategic motives, suggesting that purging the Party leadership allowed him to remove all potential rivals (including Kirov, who, according to one enduring conspiracy theory, was murdered by Stalin himself). In the shadow of impending war, purging would also ensure that the Soviet ranks were loyal. As J. Arch Getty and Oleg Naumov have argued, the Purges represented Stalin's 'fierce determination to root out all sources of real or imagined disloyalty'.[66]

For those examining the purges from a social perspective, however, the events of 1937 are seen less as evidence of Stalin's Manichean motives than as a symptom of the chaos in society following his five-year-plans, particularly the need to find scapegoats to blame for failures to meet industrial targets: 'local show trials were a convenient alternative to explaining the systemic causes of underfulfillment'.[67]

More petty motives can also be adduced. Sheila Fitzpatrick and Wendy Goldman have shown that fear, personal animosity, professional feuds and even naked self-interest led neighbours and colleagues to turn on each other and submit formal denunciations to the authorities. Peasants, in particular, used the theatre of local show trials to exact revenge against hated collective farm bosses, falling back on older, pre-revolutionary understandings of justice. Under torture, those accused would often point the finger at imagined co-conspirators, leading to yet more arrests.

So what do the Purges tell us about Stalinist society? In many ways, they fit into the broader ideological goal to foster an ideal society, representing the dark side of the modernist project to 'build socialism' that had been celebrated in the Stalin Constitution only a year before. Order No.00447 specifically targeted those who did not fit the model of an ideal 'New Soviet Person': kulaks, former prisoners, surviving members of tsarist elites (known as the byvshie liudi, or 'former people'), former Mensheviks and common criminals. As such, argues Paul Hagenloh, the Purges targeted those who 'did not or could not fit into the emerging Stalinist system'.[68] Even the practice of purging revealed the attitudes and preoccupations of the state. While they conducted what appeared to be summary justice, the NKVD worked to collate volumes of written information, including diaries, and extract elaborate confessions from the accused, a practice that represented what Jochen Hellbeck calls 'a large-scale project of classification conceived for the pursuit of irrefutable truth regarding the state of individuals' souls'.[69]

The idea of identifying enemies and removing them from society was nothing new, of course. It had been present from the birth of the Soviet state, understood in Marxist terms as a tactic of 'class struggle'. The Bolshevik determination to build a new world was dependent on the destruction of the old one and its representatives: priests, nobles and capitalist fat cats were amongst those expelled or killed during and after the revolution. The Civil War, in particular, was notorious for its turn to terror, with the entire Bolshevik leadership calling for violence to root out oppositionists: Lenin, we must remember, was ready to 'hang (hang without fail, so the people see) no fewer than one hundred known kulaks, rich men, blood suckers'. Stalin had demonstrated throughout his career that he was prepared to be the 'hard man' needed to carry out such unsavoury acts, but his propensity for violence was not unusual in the context of the revolution and its aftermath. This propensity to identify enemies and remove them through violent means took on a truly mass scale with the collectivisation process, which saw millions of peasants expropriated, executed, or sent to the Gulag.

This was not simply a case of genocidal elimination. Those enemies who were not immediately killed were provided a potential path back to inclusion in Soviet society through the Gulag, an institution which combined violent destruction and inhumane conditions with the promise of individual redemption.

Even as the Gulag camps created the conditions for millions people to die of starvation, accident or prisoner violence, society in the camps mirrored the ideological concerns and preoccupations of broader Soviet society, with inmates encouraged to reforge themselves through political education and socialist labour in anticipation of release. Indeed, the participation of Gulag inmates in the project of building socialism was not just symbolic: many of the great construction sites of the 1930s, such as Magnitogorsk and the Belomor Canal, were built by inmate labour, a fact that was initially widely celebrated in Soviet propaganda (although narratives of the Gulag would disappear from public view at the height of the Purges). 'Exploitation, oppression and mass death,' says Stephen Barnes, 'coexisted with re-education, redemption and mass release' in the Gulag system.[70]

Yet 1937 revealed significant shifts in the Soviet definition and treatment of the enemy. No longer was the definition of an enemy solely based on class. Now it was something more elemental. And now there was less belief in redemption than in the necessity of permanent removal of the enemy threat. Despite the claims of the Stalin Constitution that class divisions had been overcome and that Soviet society had entered a phase of political and social consolidation, the experience of the Purges revealed the existence of numerous social fault-lines that fed the violence of the mass repressions.

This was particularly true in relation to the 'national operations' of 1937-38, which targeted those ethnic minorities viewed as inherently susceptible to foreign influence. While the decision to target particular national minorities, such as Poles, Germans and Koreans, was framed in terms of Soviet rhetoric about class enemies and the defence of socialism – particularly in the borderlands, where the Soviet Union was seen as vulnerable to capitalist incursion – the result was the mass deportation and shootings of people purely on the basis of their ethnic background, a practice that sat very uncomfortably with the USSR's public commitment to promoting ethnic minorities within its territories. Stalin's own growing xenophobia was not incidental to this policy: as Bogdan Musial has shown, he annotated reports on the progress of the Polish operation with 'Very good! Kick and exterminate the Polish spy-filth! Annihilate it in the interest of the USSR'.[71] This practice of ethnic cleansing would continue with deadly effects into World War II.

These hatreds were fostered by a particular kind of paranoia that intensified in the context of rising international tensions. The belief that the Soviet apparatus had been infiltrated by spies, wreckers and foreign agents was a powerful framework through which to understand the world: both the traumas and upheavals of the 'Great Breakthrough', and the dangers of impending war. Stalin, whom Martin Malia has described as 'cruel to the point of sadism, and suspicious to the point of paranoia', perpetuated this paranoia in his speeches and newspaper articles calling for 'vigilance', and engineered the show trials to highlight specific dangers facing the Soviet state.[72] It is likely that he believed in these dangers. As he remarked to a group of hero-workers at a Kremlin reception in October 1937:

I'm not even sure that everyone present, I truly apologise to you, is for the people… there might be people who are working for the Soviet government but at the same time have set themselves up with some intelligence agency in the West.[73]

Given all these complexities and contradictions, it is perhaps unsurprising that the purges were not understood as a genocide at the time. Looking back at the year 1937 in his powerful history of the Terror, *The Gulag Archipelago*, Aleksandr Solzhenitsyn explained:

How could we know anything about those arrests and why should we think about them? Two or three professors had been arrested, but after all they hadn't been our dancing partners, and it might even be easier to pass our exams as a result. Twenty-year-olds, we marched in the ranks of those born the year the Revolution took place, and because we were the same age as the Revolution, the brightest of futures lay ahead. [74]

Even those caught up in the machine of terror found ways to rationalise it, seeking to blame themselves or their loved ones for doing something wrong, or even accepting that the innocent might have to die for the longed-for communist world to come into being. In his last letter to Stalin, even as he protested his innocence and begged for his life, Nikolai Bukharin wrote:

> there is something great and bold about the political idea of a general purge … For God's sake, don't think that I am engaging here in reproaches, even in my inner thoughts. I know all too well that great plans, great ideas, and great interests take precedence over everything.[75]

Yet the results were catastrophic. While Soviet death rates are not without controversy (estimates of deaths from the Purges range up to 20 million), we know from recently declassified files that, over the course of a year and a half, 1.6 million people were arrested and 700,000 shot. This equates to 1,500 killed per day. Those who escaped execution and reached the Gulag faced such inhospitable conditions that millions died: 90,564 in 1938 alone. The Purges severely affected Soviet institutions: 78 percent of the Party's 1934 Central Committee were arrested and shot; the army lost its general, Marshal Tukhachevskii, and one half of its officer corps; the loss of experienced economists (and the reluctance amongst those who remained to propose any changes that might later be considered 'sabotage') caused a decline in industrial growth. They also ripped apart social bonds, causing neighbour to fear neighbour, and tearing families apart.

In their later accounts of the period, Stalin and his inner circle affirmed that the Purges were a necessary procedure, one that unfortunately spiralled out of control due to the 'excesses' of the NKVD head Nikolai Ezhov, whom Stalin referred to as 'a beast! A degenerate' (a reference to Ezhov's widely rumoured bisexuality). According to Molotov's reminiscences:

> 1937 was necessary. If you consider that after the revolution we were slashing left and right, and we were victorious, but enemies of different sorts remained, and in the face of the impending danger of fascist aggression they might unite. We owe the fact that we did not have a fifth column during the war to '37.[76]

Maintaining the need for the Purges, and blaming its atrocities on Ezhov, allowed Stalin to wind them down and maintain his own authority; he had Ezhov removed from his position in 1939 and shot in 1940, having found him guilty of leading a counter-revolutionary organisation within the NKVD. This shifting of responsibility was broadly successful: many believed that Stalin did not know what Ezhov was doing, and wrote desperate petitions asking him to intervene to spare their lives and those of their loved ones. The Purges are known in Russian as the 'Ezhovshchina', and its atrocities were not attributed to Stalin until after his death.

CHAPTER TWELVE

A WARTIME LEADER

In 1945, Stalin took his place alongside Winston Churchill and Franklin D. Roosevelt in the garden of Yalta's Livadiia Palace, as the 'big three' proclaimed victory over Nazi Germany and established the peacetime division of Europe. In the context of the ensuing Cold War, however, and the revelation of Stalin's crimes in Khrushchev's Secret Speech, this equating of Stalin with his western wartime counterparts began to be seen as something of an embarrassment. Was Stalin really a wartime leader equal to Churchill?

Stalin's role in the Second World War – or the Great Patriotic War, as it is known in Russia – was complex. Following the shock invasion of the USSR by Nazi troops in 1941, it is certainly possible to argue that Stalin's actions had made a bad situation considerably worse. The Purges had severely weakened the military leadership. The loss of Marshal Tukhachevskii and the more competent specialists in the military ranks meant that there were few who understood military tactics and could advise Stalin. The decimation of the officer corps had destroyed the chain of command, making the passing of orders to the rank and file particularly difficult. In the vital hours after the invasion, the leadership lacked the mechanisms to put their plans into action; the plans themselves were also unclear.

In 1939, to the general consternation of the Soviet people, Stalin had signed a pact of non-aggression with the Nazi leadership, promising ten years of peaceful cooperation between the two, and – secretly – establishing the border between the Soviet and German spheres of influence, which established the framework for Soviet troops to invade and occupy eastern Poland, which they did in September 1939. The Molotov-Ribbentrop Pact, as it was known, was a tactical move to gain breathing space in the face of war, and a means to expand Soviet territory and influence into Eastern Europe. As Timothy Snyder has shown, it also revealed an affinity between Hitler and Stalin. Both men had, in Stalin's words, 'a common desire to get rid of the old equilibrium', and both saw the destruction of Poland as a key step in the expansion of their respective regimes.[77] As a result, however, the German invasion came as a shock to all, Stalin included.

The enduring rumour has it that on 22nd June 1941, as Operation Barbarossa saw Nazi troops sweep into Soviet territory, Stalin went AWOL for several days. The reality was not quite so dramatic, but the first weeks of war certainly saw a vacuum at the top of the leadership. Placing his faith in the pact with Germany had been a supreme miscalculation, and the shock was such that Stalin did not know what to do. He refused to believe that this was an invasion, interpreting it instead as a 'provocation' on the part of German troops, and ordered the Soviet army not to retaliate.

When he learned that war had been declared, according to Marshal Zhukov, he 'silently dropped into his chair and became immersed in thought. A long and painful pause ensued.' He refused to talk to the country, leaving it to Molotov to make the radio announcement that Russia was at war. All orders in the first days were signed by Timoshenko, Malenkov and Zhukov, while Stalin refused to take charge at Command Headquarters, remaining in his dacha and declining to come to the Kremlin. This indecisiveness, especially in light of his political dominance in the years before the war, caused unease in the leadership and the country.

On the back of this bad start, the first months of war were catastrophic. In the first six months, the Germans captured 3,355,000 Soviet prisoners of war and occupied most of the European part of the USSR. This only intensified Stalin's depression; on learning that Minsk had fallen, he remarked that 'Lenin has left us a great legacy. We, his heirs, have pissed it all away.' Yet the essence of Stalinism, with its central control, reliance on mass enthusiasm, and lack of respect for human life, enabled the tide to turn. Once the shock had worn off, the Stalinist machine swung into action, setting up a State Defence Committee, headed by Stalin, to oversee the war effort. People and industries were evacuated to the east, including 2,592 of Russia's new factories, which were moved to Central Asia, the Volga, Siberia and the Urals.

The command economy allowed industry to move quickly to

the production of armaments; as Mark Harrison has shown, a children's bicycle factory 'started making flame throwers' while 'at a die-stamping plant teaspoons and paperclips gave way to entrenching tools and parts for anti-tank grenades'.[78] Soviet workers again pushed to overfulfil their production quotas, under the mobilisation slogan: 'all for the front, all for victory!' With these supreme efforts, the tide of the war began to turn.

Stalin's public persona also underwent a dramatic change. His first speech to Soviet citizens did not contain his usual Marxist references, but instead called on the bonds of friendship and family, addressing 'Comrades! Citizens! Brothers and sisters! My friends'. Patriotic, distinctly Russian imagery was invoked to cement this notion of collective struggle; for the first time since the Revolution, the term 'fatherland' returned to public discourse. In November 1941, he announced:

The war you are waging is a war of liberation, a just war. May you be inspired in this war by the heroic figures of our great ancestors, Aleksandr Nevskii, Dmitrii Donskoi, Minin and Pozharskii, Aleksandr Suvorov, Mikhail Kutuzov. May you be blessed by great Lenin's victorious banner. Death to the German invaders![79]

One could argue that this was Stalin's only possible response to the unfolding situation. The everyday experiences of Soviet citizens reinforced the belief that this was a struggle for national survival. In the ethnic worldview of the Nazis, Soviet citizens were Slavs, a species of subhuman, and Nazi troops were encouraged to rape and brutalise.

It is important to note that there was some significant Soviet collaboration with the Nazi occupiers, such as the volunteer army established by captured Soviet commander Andrei Vlasov to fight the Red Army, or tens of thousands of Ukrainians who joined the partisan movement in opposition to the Soviet regime that had forced their collectivisation and brought about the famine of 1932-33. Given the brutality of Stalinist policies, particularly in the Western borderlands, this was perhaps to be expected. Yet any lingering sense that German rule might be better than Stalinism was shattered by Nazi brutality, which reached its apogee in the three-year blockade of Leningrad, where an estimated one million people died from shelling and starvation. It is unsurprising that those who experienced Nazi atrocities were keen to see their struggle as a war of liberation for an ancient and glorious country.

In many respects, Soviet public culture accepted that the war was a collective effort, downplaying Stalin's cult of personality in favour of everyday heroes. Soviet citizens performed great feats of daring, particularly in the occupied territories, to repel the invading forces, forming partisan units behind enemy lines to resist the invader. One figurehead of the partisan movement was the young woman Zoia Kosmodemianskaia, who was captured by Nazi forces behind enemy lines and hanged as a traitor. In a challenge to Stalin's prudish tastes, her naked corpse was pictured on the pages of *Pravda*, and she was (and is) widely considered a martyr. In an attempt further to promote this sense of collectivism, the Russian Orthodox Church was again allowed to operate openly; the surprising speed with which church institutions were re-established, in both the occupied and unoccupied territories, raises the question of how far atheism (and other official Soviet values) had really taken hold in Soviet society before the war.

There were other factors, too, that contributed to Soviet victory. The alliance between Britain, the United States and the USSR proved decisive, providing the Soviet army with approximately $10 billion in Lend Lease aid, including tanks, planes, and grain. Stalin's role in the international community was pivotal here; both Churchill and Roosevelt were convinced that he was an honest and trustworthy ally. Stalin was even named *Time* Magazine's Man of the Year in 1941. The sheer size of the Soviet army, and the number of reservists on which to draw, was also critical (as had been the case in many previous Russian wars). Along the border, for example, Soviet forces outnumbered the Germans by 1.5:1. These factors, and the heroic effort made by ordinary Soviet citizens, allowed them to turn the tide of war at the epic battle of Stalingrad and push the invader back to Berlin.

Was it right, then, to thank Stalin for his role in the victory? On balance, perhaps it was. Over the course of the war, he had become a formidable and experienced military ruler. He certainly made bad mistakes – not least the 1939 pact with Hitler that contributed to the strength of Nazi Germany and the likelihood of war – but his willingness to study and his meticulous and involved style of leadership lent itself well to the pressures of the war effort. As Marshal Vasilevskii wrote, by the end of the war 'Stalin was thinking in terms of modern warfare and grasped all the issues involved in preparing and conducting operations'.[80]

Yet it was not his victory alone. The Soviet leadership, and the Soviet people, had suffered and sacrificed in order to defeat the invader. Indeed, it is possible to argue that they had suffered substantially more due to Stalin's policies. The infamous Order

No.227, which exhorted soldiers and commanders to take 'Not one step back!' and established penal detachments behind the frontline to shoot them if they retreated (an echo of a similar Nazi policy), intensified the casualties. Even as the tide of war turned decisively in Russia's favour, Stalin engaged in the forced imprisonment and deportation of a number of ethnic groups, including the Kalmyks, Crimean Tatars, and some North Caucasian ethnic groups, to Kazakhstan and Central Asia; of the million who were deported, hundreds of thousands perished on the way. For Gulag prisoners considered too dangerously anti-Soviet to be released to fight the invader, the war was particularly lethal: one in four prisoners died of starvation in 1942 alone. There were few families in the postwar Russia that had not been touched by death, either at the hands of the Nazi troops, or as a result of these repressive Stalinist policies.

As the war wound down, however, the machinery of Stalin's cult moved back into action, airbrushing out the efforts of ordinary people in favour of the leading hand of the *vozhd*, who was now given the title of Generalissimo. As Molotov proclaimed:

In the difficult years of war, the Red Army and Soviet people were guided by the wise and experienced *vozhd* of the Soviet Union, the great Stalin. In the name of Generalissimo Stalin, the glorious victories of our army will go down in the history of our country and in world history.

Following their years of struggle, however, it was not entirely clear that the Soviet people would accept this appropriation of their victory.

CHAPTER THIRTEEN

THE LAST YEARS

In many ways, the period between the declaration of victory in 1945 and Stalin's death in 1953 can be seen as the apotheosis of his leadership. Victory had legitimised the system he had built. As one veteran wrote,

> Drunk with the conceit of victory, we decided that our system was ideal… and we not only neglected to improve it, but, on the contrary, we grew ever more dogmatic about it.[81]

Within the leadership, this triumph – both real and symbolic – was widely celebrated, particularly in the demonstration of military might on Red Square in the victory parade of June 1945. It also forestalled any attempt at reform. As Robert Service puts it, in 1945 'Stalin's mind was a stopped clock'.[82]

The clock of Stalin's mind had stopped, but his policies had not – far from it. The extension of Soviet power into Eastern Europe provided fertile new territories for Stalinist policies. The Red Army and the NKVD, assisted by local communists who were promoted to positions of power, employed Stalinist measures to 'Sovietize' these countries and their populations, using the tried and tested combination of violence (the targeting of class 'enemies' and ethnic cleansing), and enthusiasm (the creation of Soviet institutions and mass propaganda drives). They also attempted to impose Soviet economic structures on these countries, particularly collectivisation, which was resisted as forcefully in Eastern Europe as it had been in the USSR. These policies combined with the legacy of German destruction and a disastrous drought to provoke another famine which devastated the region in 1946-47.

This period of 'high' or 'late' Stalinism, however, concealed a number of shifts in the leadership and in Soviet society more broadly, that undermined his authority. During the war, when he had been personally involved in all military decisions, the running of the country had been increasingly delegated to government bodies, such as the Politburo, and to those in his immediate circle. Oleg Khlevniuk writes:

Whatever assignments were given to these top leaders, under the pressures of war and by sheer necessity they operated with significant administrative latitude. What mattered were results.[83]

In stark contrast to the paranoia of the 1930s, the Soviet leadership during the war functioned on trust and a measure of autonomy. This did not mean that Stalin's dominance was directly challenged, but necessity required a turn to collective leadership. Following victory, it was not so easy for him to rein in the ambitions and influence of his colleagues. In October 1945, he went on holiday – his first in nine years – and the Western press immediately seized on this as evidence that his leadership was over and a power struggle for the succession was taking place.

If the leadership had changed, so too had the populace. Elena Zubkova has shown that Soviet citizens after the war had a new set of expectations. The suffering and destruction experienced during the conflict, and the famine that followed it, caused citizens to yearn for the post-war rewards of a stable, good life. Yet, increasingly, the reality of Soviet life did not meet their expectations. This disappointment was exacerbated by the fact that the displacements of the war had allowed many Soviet citizens to go beyond the borders of the USSR for the first time. Experiencing 'capitalism' first hand, these veterans and prisoners of war were shocked to discover that, far from being poor and unequal, life in these countries was materially better than the system they had endured in the 1930s. While Stalin continued to mobilise Soviet citizens, praising them as the 'decisive force that secured a historic victory against an enemy of humanity', they were demanding material rewards – such as healthcare, housing and consumer goods – for their sufferings.

The internal instabilities that followed the victory were more than matched by external instabilities and the developing Cold War. By 1945, even as the allies were cooperating on matters of security, Stalin's mistrust of the West had begun to grow. Determined to maintain Soviet interests in Eastern Europe and Japan, Stalin provoked the Western leadership, who – despite their continued belief that Stalin was an honest and pragmatic politician – were concerned about the occupation of Eastern European nations by the Red Army. Equally, America's display of nuclear might at Hiroshima and Nagasaki in 1945 made the Soviet leadership fearful that an all-out assault on the world's first socialist state was in the offing. The development of the Cold War was prolonged and complex, arising as much out of deep-seated ideological world views as concrete actions, but it was unclear at first whether 'hot' war would not soon resume.

As he grappled with these issues, it is important to note that Stalin,

Stalin and Mao met in 1949. They had a strained relationship, disagreeing about the future of communism

too, was a different man. In 1945, he was 67, and had been leader for 17 years. His health was poor; during the war, he had suffered repeat-edly from bad bouts of influenza and developed a heart problem. He suffered from atherosclerosis and rheumatism. These were not helped by his sedentary lifestyle and his fondness for entertaining; his doctors advised him to cut down on his drinking and not to drink on Sun-days. His health had an inevitable impact on his behaviour. After his death, one of the doctors who examined his body reported:

> I believe that Stalin's cruelty and suspiciousness, his fear of enemies and loss of the ability to assess people and events, his extreme obstinacy – all this was the result…of athero-sclerosis of the arteries in his brain… Basically, the state was being governed by a sick man.[84]

Frustrated by his physical weaknesses, Stalin tried to put things back the way they had been before the war. To cement his dicta-torship, he shook up the leadership, lashing out at Molotov (his *de facto* deputy) and forcing him to grovel for his position, and expel-ling Marshal Zhukov, the leader of the victorious army, from the Central Committee. To limit the influence of returning prison-ers of war, he ordered them to be immediately taken into custody and sent to the Gulag. Old economic systems were reinstated; a new five-year plan was formulated in 1946, with the usual high targets for heavy industry and raw materials: 500 million tons of coal, 60 million tons of steel and 60 million tons of petroleum. As many historians have shown, these plans and targets had limited effectiveness, and Soviet citizens continued to push for a more lib-eral political sphere, and a measure of the good life. Juliane Fürst argues that 'late Stalinism was as much about reinvention as it was about reconstruction'.[85]

As a last resort, Stalin returned to his previous techniques of violence and purging. Three cases dominated the late Stalinist period: the Zhdanovshchina, a campaign against Western influences in science and the arts; the 1949 Leningrad Affair, which saw prominent Party leaders in Leningrad accused of embezzling state funds to set up a rival power base to Moscow; and the 1952 Doctors' Plot, in which nine Kremlin doctors were accused of conspiring to murder Party leaders. Historians have read these campaigns as an attempt by the Soviet regime to restore order following the chaos of war, and, in the words of Fürst, to 'gain or regain control of this most elusive entity of Soviet life – the Soviet mind'.[86] In addition, these cases all had a decidedly anti-Semitic bent. In the context of the developing Cold War, Jewish citizens were seen to have divided loyalties, and the accused doctors (six of whom were Jewish) were said to be part of a wider American-Jewish plot. Historians believe that the Doctors' Plot was the opening salvo in what would become a major purge of the Party leadership. It is not hard to imagine what might have happened if death had not intervened.

CHAPTER FOURTEEN

DEATH OF A GOD

For a man who had wielded such power, Stalin suffered an ignominious end. On 28th February 1953, following his usual tradition, Stalin dined and watched a film with his closest associates, the 'Big Four' of Malenkov, Beria, Khrushchev and Bulganin. The evening was typically raucous and drunken. In the early hours of the morning, as his guests left, Stalin told his bodyguards that he was turning in and wanted not to be disturbed.

By mid-morning on 1st March, when he had not emerged to ask for his usual cup of tea, the bodyguards were starting to get nervous. The consequences of disobeying a direct order were well understood, however, so no one dared knock on the door and check on him. At 6.30 pm, to everyone's relief, a light was switched on in the dacha. Yet Stalin still did not emerge. At 10pm, when a package of documents from the Central Committee was delivered, the decision was made to brave the ruler's displeasure and enter. The bodyguards found him slumped on the floor in his own urine, having suffered a stroke.

The events of the following few hours provide rich material for farce, as Armando Iannucci's 2017 film *The Death of Stalin* has recently demonstrated (although the film was, perhaps inevitably, banned in Russia). Given Stalin's reputation, however, the actions of the Soviet leadership are all too understandable. Word was sent to the 'Big Four', who arrived at the dacha in the early hours of 2nd March. They consulted at length with the bodyguards, trying to decide if they should go in to check on Stalin, but were constrained by their fear of the retaliation that might ensue if they saw him in such a humiliating physical state and he recovered. Beria and Malenkov went in (Malenkov in his stockinged feet, as his shoes squeaked). Stalin appeared to be sleeping, so the two beat a hasty retreat, telling the bodyguards that he was fine.

As a result, it was many hours before Stalin was seen by a doctor, who diagnosed a clear case of cerebral haemorrhage. The question of treatment was problematic. No one wanted to act without care and skill, but the nine most prominent doctors in the country had recently been arrested as part of the 'Doctor's Plot'. According to Robert Service, the imprisoned doctors were consulted for their opinion on Stalin's symptoms – paralysis and vomiting blood – which they pronounced as 'grave'. Coming on the heels of prolonged torture, this consultation must have been a surreal

Members of the cast of The Death of Stalin. *Khrushchev is second from the right.*

experience.

As Stalin's condition worsened, the political machinery of state swung into action. A report was made to the Central Committee on the state of his health on 4th March. As family members and colleagues gathered round his bedside, the Party leadership voted to create a new Presidium, thus re-establishing collective leadership. His formal titles were divided up: Malenkov became Chairman of the Council of Ministers and Khrushchev became Secretary of the Central Committee. The session ended at 8.40 p.m.; at 9.50, Stalin died.

Many were suspicious about the circumstances of his death, among them Molotov, who had recently fallen out of favour with Stalin and was not present at the dacha: 'Stalin did not die a natural death,' he said later. 'He wasn't seriously ill. He was working steadily… and he remained very spry.' Molotov viewed Beria, the head of the NKVD, as the most likely candidate for his murder. Indeed, a BBC documentary *Who Killed Stalin?*, which aired in 2005, set out a convoluted conspiracy theory that strongly implicated Beria. Yet, as Christopher Read has written,

> no evidence exists to support such a theory … It is in the
> nature of strokes to come out of the blue and there is little
> doubt that it was a stroke that killed Stalin.[87]

Stalin had left orders to be embalmed, like his friend and teacher, Lenin. This was more complicated than it might have been as Boris Zbarskii, the chief scientist in charge of the embalming laboratory, had been arrested in 1952. The procedure was completed rapidly, however, and from 6th March, the body lay in state in the Hall of Columns, across from the Kremlin. So many ordinary citizens came to pay their respects that they caused a stampede; hundreds were crushed to death – Stalin's last massacre. He was laid to rest in the mausoleum next to Lenin, the holy of holies at the centre of the Soviet state.

As his problematic legacy became subject to official debate, the location of his embalmed corpse was called into question. In 1961, five years after Stalin was denounced by Khrushchev in his Secret Speech, his body was quietly removed from the mausoleum in the middle of the night and buried along the Kremlin wall. A modest monument was installed in 1970. While the decision was never officially explained to the Soviet people, says Polly Jones, its symbolism was clear:

> Stalin's removal from the mausoleum was not only a way to
> address the 'incongruity' with the 'holy' Lenin, but it was
> also a way to perform his 'guilt' and 'responsibility' for the
> heinous crimes of the period. As one Moscow plant man-

ager explained, the 'logic' of the decision derived from the guilt of Stalin 'on whose conscience is the blood of thousands of innocent people'.[88]

Stalin with his successor, Nikita Khrushchev

CHAPTER FIFTEEN

STALIN'S LEGACY

Since Stalin's death, the assessment of his rule has shifted according to the prevailing political winds. The glorification of his leadership was struck a decisive blow in 1956, when his successor Nikita Khrushchev denounced him and publicly acknowledged the atrocities of his leadership. His 'Secret Speech' was part of a broader move away from Stalin's model of leadership, involving the mass amnesties of prisoners from the Gulag, the bringing of the NKVD under Party control, and the establishment of practices of communal leadership.

The speech questioned Stalin's legitimacy, citing key passages from Lenin's Testament and including letters from his victims, pleading for their lives. Within Soviet society, it led to a spontaneous outburst of iconoclasm, as statues and paintings of Stalin were torn down, his works were pulped, cities and institutions bearing his name were renamed and citizens were encouraged to speak and write openly of the traumas of the Stalinist past.

Yet, as Miriam Dobson has explained,

> even as the new leaders sought to break with many of the practices developed under Stalin, they were constantly aware that sweeping condemnation of the past might undermine the legitimacy of communist rule.[89]

Khrushchev himself walked a careful line with the Secret Speech, criticising Stalin's actions in the Party purges and during the Second World War, but framing the 'victories' of collectivisation, industrialisation and war (and the attendant national repressions and brutal famines) as beyond reproach. That Stalin's successors were implicated in the crimes of his rule was sometimes baldly stated, as in the poem 'Stalin's Heirs' by the celebrated young poet Evgenii Evtushenko, published in 1962:

> Let some repeat over and over:
> 'Relax!' – I cannot be calm.
> As long as Stalin's heirs exist on earth
> It will seem to me
> that Stalin is still in the Mausoleum.[90]

Indeed, one of the most worrying expressions of iconoclasm during the de-Stalinization campaign, the tearing down of Stalin's statue in Budapest, marked the beginning of the Hungarian uprising of 1956, which challenged Soviet rule in Eastern Europe. During the late Soviet period, the leadership was torn between the desire to repudiate Stalin, and the concern that he was too intimately associated with the foundations of the Soviet state to challenge his legitimacy directly. For all its problems, the cult of personality was supremely successful in associating Stalin with the victories of the Soviet regime. The return to commemorating the Second World War under Brezhnev had the inevitable result of rehabilitating Stalin to a certain degree: his official birthday in was marked with an editorial in *Pravda* in 1969.

Yet this partial rehabilitation could not stem the tide of criticism that had been unleashed under Khrushchev, and attempts to silence critics only pushed them underground. During the Brezhnev era, key dissident figures – writing from a variety of ideological positions – focused their criticisms of Soviet socialism on the figure of Stalin, who represented, in the words of Roy Medvedev, a 'serious disease' from which the USSR was yet to recover.[91] For many, the disease of Stalinism did not invalidate the utopian visions of the revolution, but the difference between these visions and Stalinist reality was stark.

As Andrei Siniavskii, writing under the pseudonym Abram Terz, explained:

So that prisons should vanish forever, we built new prisons... So that not one drop of blood be shed any more, we killed and killed and killed.[92]

These works were censored and their authors exiled and imprisoned, yet their ideas continued to circulate through practices of self-publication (samizdat) and publication abroad (tamizdat), fuelling the rise of the international human rights movement.

During the dramatic upheavals of Gorbachev's campaign of glasnost, or 'openness', in the late 1980s, the crimes of Stalinism took centre stage. Gorbachev's initial intention had been to encourage criticisms of the recent Soviet past in order to lay the groundwork for reforms – his view was 'there were mistakes, and serious ones, but the country moved forward' – yet the unprecedented discussion in the public sphere inevitably turned to Stalin. 'Professional historians waged their own battle over the interpretation of the Soviet past, and Stalinism in particular, in the popular press,' says Kathleen Smith.

> Letters to the editor make it clear that the public was transfixed by new horrifying stories about the fate of purge victims and by artistic works that dealt with moral problems raised during and as a consequence of Stalinism.[93]

The emotive power of Stalinist history had a decisive impact on the progress of the glasnost campaign, and on the eventual collapse of the USSR. The August coup of 1991, which saw a group of hard-line communists attempt to halt Gorbachev's reforms by force and led directly to the final collapse of the Soviet regime, was seen as harking back to Stalinist repression; one eyewitness said he felt 'Stalin's ghost' at his shoulder.

During and after the Soviet collapse, a human rights organisation called Memorial played a key role in the re-assessment of Stalin and the recording of his political repression. Memorial began life as a regional, grass-roots movement, lobbying for a memorial to Stalin's victims, which was finally erected in central Moscow in 1990. After 1991, when the impetus to protect the narrative of Soviet superiority disappeared, it acquired national prominence. Memorial's key publishing project, the Leningrad Martyrology, contains lists of victims and studies of individual purge cases. This focus on individual repressions inevitably shifted the focus away from Stalin's great projects and victories to the minutiae of the lives he destroyed.

The image of Stalin was also explored in new and unexpected ways in literature of the 1990s, when the ending of censorship allowed for alternative viewpoints to be expressed. Rosalind Marsh has explored how the carefully constructed persona of the *vozhd* was destroyed by the postmodernist experimentation of writers like Vladimir Sorokin, who portrayed Stalin as a clone who engages in a homosexual affair with a clone of Khrushchev in the novel *Blue Lard*. Later in the 1990s, historical fiction focused on the Stalin's private life and personality. A novel by Anatolii Marchenko, *Stalin: The Dictator* 'draws conventional comparisons between dictatorship and demonic power, referring to the Last Judgement and the coming of the Antichrist'.[94]

Yet public opinion did not decisively move towards condemnation. In 2003, a poll found that 47 percent of Russians had a positive or neutral view of Stalin. Ten years later, a poll by the Carnegie foundation revealed that over half of Russian respondents viewed Stalin as a 'wise leader who brought the Soviet Union to might and prosperity'.

Much of this continued popularity is down to the leadership of Vladimir Putin, whose push to reinstate a centralised and controlled state structure has encouraged positive assessments of Stalin. As Maria Lipman has commented in response to the Carnegie poll:

> The overwhelming significance of the war and of Stalin as the commander in chief who led the nation to victory is one piece of the Stalin puzzle, one explanation why unambiguous condemnation of him is impossible in Russia. In Putin's Russia, Stalin remains the embodiment of the state at its most powerful.[95]

Condemnation of Stalin is not forbidden in the new Russia, although organisations such as Memorial have found their activities sharply curtailed. New histories and textbooks dealing with Stalin tend, in the words of Khlevniuk, towards 'pseudo-scholarly apologias'.[96] These works acknowledge the trauma and violence of the Stalin era, but present it as the necessary birth pangs of a strong, modern Russia; equally, they insist that Stalinist modernity, even in its most illiberal, statist form, is still better than anything Western liberal democracies can offer. On 9th May, when Red Square is filled with veterans celebrating Victory Day, it is not Stalin the monster whose presence is felt. It is Stalin the Generalissimo, victor and father of a people.

END NOTES

A BRIEF CHRONOLOGY

1878 Iosif Vissarionovich Dzhugashvili born in Gori, Georgia.

1894 Enrols in Tiflis Seminary. Exposure to Marxist teachings.

1898 Joins local Marxist organisation.

1902 Stalin's first arrest.

1903 Russian Social Democratic Workers' Party splits into two factions, Bolsheviks and Mensheviks

1906 Marries Ekaterina Svarnidze (one son, Yakov).

1912 Joins Bolshevik Central Committee.

1913 Publishes *Marxism and the National Question*. Begins to use pseudonym of Stalin. Arrest and exile to Siberia, affair with Lidia Pereprygina.

1917 Two revolutions shake Russia. The first, in February, forces the Tsar to abdicate in favour of a Provisional Government. The second, in October, sees the Bolshevik Party seize power and declare the foundation of a workers' state. Stalin is declared People's Commissar of Nationalities.

1919 Marries Nadezhda Allilueva (two children, Vasilii and Svetlana).

1919-1921 Civil war in Russia. Stalin sent to Tsaritsyn to acquire grain for the war effort.

1922 Stalin appointed General Secretary of the Communist Party. Dictation of Lenin's *Testament.*

1924 Death of Lenin.

1926 Expulsion of Trotsky, Zinoviev and Kamenev from the Politburo.

1928 First Five Year Plan announced; collectivisation of agriculture and industrialisation campaign.

1929 Stalin's official fiftieth birthday. The Stalin Cult begins.

1932 Suicide of Nadezhda Allilueva.

1934 Assassination of Sergei Kirov.

1935 First show trial of Zinoviev and Kamenev.

1936 New law against abortion passed. Second show trial of Zinoviev and Kamenev, who are convicted and shot.

1937 Attach on Shostakovich's opera *Lady Macbeth of Mtsensk*. Show trial of Radek, Piatakov. Purges of army officers, height of 'Ezhovshchina'.

1938 Show trial of Bukharin and Radek. Purges wind down.

1939 Molotov-Ribbentrop pact of non-aggression with Germany is signed.

1941 Germany invades Soviet Union. War is declared.

1945 Yalta conference, war ends. United States drops atom bomb on Hiroshima.

1946 Churchill's 'Iron Curtain' speech. Beginning of Zhadanovshchina.

1948 The Leningrad Affair.

1953 Announcement of the Doctors' Plot. Stalin dies on 5th March.

1956 Khrushchev's Secret Speech, start of the de-Stalinization campaign.

1961 Stalin's body removed from Mausoleum.

BIBLIOGRAPHY

The list of published works on Stalin is vast and continues to grow; it is not possible, therefore, for me to give a comprehensive bibliography here. The following is a list of titles that I have relied upon or quoted directly.

Steven Barnes, *Death and Redemption: The Gulag and the Shaping of Soviet Society*, Princeton University Press, 2011.

David Brandenberger, *Propaganda State in Crisis: Soviet Ideology, Indoctrination, and Terror under Stalin, 1927-1941*, Yale University Press, 2011.

Kate Brown, 'Gridded Lives: Why Kazakhstan and Montana are Nearly the Same Place', *The American Historical Review*, Vol. 106, No. 1 (Feb., 2001), pp. 17-48.

Katerina Clark, *Petersburg: Crucible of Cultural Revolution*, Harvard University Press, 1995.

Sarah Davies, *Public Opinion in Stalin's Russia: Terror, Propaganda and Dissent, 1934-41*, Cambridge University Press, 1997.

Sarah Davies and James Harris, *Stalin's World: Dictating the Soviet Order*, Yale University Press, 2014.

Isaac Deutscher, *Stalin*, Oxford University Press, 1949.

Miriam Dobson, *Khrushchev's Cold Summer: Gulag Returnees, Crime, and the Fate of Reform after Stalin*, Cornell University Press, 2009.

J. Arch Getty and Oleg Naumov, *The Road to Terror: Stalin and the Self-Destruction of the Bolsheviks, 1932-39*, Yale University Press, 1999.

Wendy Goldman, *Terror and Democracy in the Age of Stalin: The Social Dynamics of Repression*, Cambridge University Press, 2007.

Mark Edele, *Stalinist Society: 1928-1953*, Oxford University Press, 2008.

Laura Engelstein, *Russia in Flames: War, Revolution, Civil War, 1914-1921*, Oxford

University Press, 2017.

Sheila Fitzpatrick, *Everyday Stalinism: Ordinary Life in Extraordinary Times: Soviet Russia in the 1930s*, Oxford University Press, 2000.

Juliane Fürst (ed.), *Late Stalinist Russia: Society between Reconstruction and Reinvention*, Routledge, 2009.

Paul Hagenloh, *Stalin's Police: Public Order and Mass Repression in the USSR, 1926-1941*, Johns Hopkins University Press, 2009.

James Harris, *The Great Fear: Stalin's Terror of the 1930s*, Oxford University Press, 2016.

Jochen Hellbeck, *Revolution on my Mind: Writing a Diary under Stalin*, Harvard University Press, 2006.

David Hoffmann, *Stalinist Values: The Cultural Norms of Soviet Modernity, 1917-1991*, Cornell University Press, 2003.

Peter Holquist, *Making War, Forging Revolution: Russia's Continuum of Crisis, 1914-1921*, Harvard University Press, 2002.

Geoffrey Hosking, *Rulers and Victims: The Russians in the Soviet Union*, Harvard University Press, 2006.

Polly Jones, *Myth, Memory, Trauma: Rethinking the Stalinist Past in the Soviet Union, 1953-70*, Yale University Press, 2013.

Oleg Khlevniuk, *Stalin: New Biography of a Dictator*, Yale University Press, 2015.

Stephen Kotkin, Stalin: *Paradoxes of Power, 1978-1928*, Allen Lane, 2014, and Stalin: Waiting for Hitler, 1929-1941, Allen Lane, 2017.

Martin Malia, *The Soviet Tragedy: A History of Socialism in Russia, 1917-1991*, Free Press, 1994.

Rosalind Marsh, *Literature, History and Identity in Post-Soviet Russia*, 1991-2006, Peter Lang, 2007.

Terry Martin, *The Affirmative Action Empire: Nations and Nationalism in the Soviet Union, 1923-1939*, Cornell University Press, 2001.

Roy Medvedev, *Let History Judge*, Macmillan, 1971.

Karen Petrone, *Life Has Become More Joyous, Comrades: Celebrations in the Time of Stalin*, Indiana University Press, 2000.

Jan Plamper, *The Stalin Cult: A Study in the Alchemy of Power*, Yale University Press, 2012.

Ethan Pollock, *Stalin and the Soviet Science Wars*, Princeton University Press, 2008.

Christopher Read, *Stalin: From the Caucasus to the Kremlin,* Routledge, 2016.

Donald Rayfield, 'Stalin as Poet', *PN Review,* Vol. 11, No. 3, January-February 1985.

Simon Sebag-Montefiore, *Young Stalin,* Phoenix, 2008, and *Stalin: The Court of the Red Tsar,* Weidenfield & Nicholson, 2003.

Robert Service, *Stalin: A Biography,* Macmillan, 2004.

Yuri Slezkine, *The House of Government: A Saga of the Russian Revolution,* Princeton University Press, 2017.

Kathleen Smith, *Mythmaking in the New Russia: Politics and Memory during the Yeltsin Era,* Cornell University Press, 2002.

Timothy Snyder, *Bloodlands: Europe between Hitler and Stalin,* Basic Books, 2010.

Aleksandr Solzhenitsyn, *The Gulag Archipelago, 1918-56,* Harvill Press, 2003.

Ronald Suny, *The Soviet Experiment: Russia, the USSR, and the Successor States,* Oxford University Press, 2010.

Nicholas Timasheff, *The Great Retreat: The Rise and Decline of Socialism in Russia,* E. P. Dutton and Co., 1946.

Abram Terz (Andrei Sinyavsky), *The Trial Begins, and, On Socialist Realism,* University of California Press, 1992.

Leon Trotsky, Stalin: *An Appraisal of the Man and his Influence,* MacGibbon and Kee, 1968.

Leon Trotsky, *The Revolution Betrayed: What is the Soviet Union and Where Is It Going?,* Doubleday, Doran & Company, Inc., 1937.

Lynne Viola, *Peasant Rebels under Stalin: Collectivisation and the Culture of Peasant Resistance,* Oxford University Press, 1996.

Thomas De Waal, Maria Lipman, Lev Gudkov and Lasha Bakradze, *The Stalin Puzzle: Deciphering Post-Soviet Public Opinion,* Carnegie Endowment for International Peace, 2013.

Serhy Yekelchyk, *Stalin's Citizens: Everyday Politics in the Wake of Total War,* Oxford University Press, 2014.

Elena Zubkova, *Russia after the War: Hopes, Illusions, and Disappointments, 1945-1957,* M. E. Sharpe, 1998.

Seventeen Moments in Soviet History: www.soviethistory.msu.edu

Marxists Internet Archive: www.marxists.org

END NOTES

November 7, 1929: http://soviethistory. msu.edu/1929-2/year-of-great-change/ year-of-great-change-texts/a-year-of-great-change/

22 Suny, *Soviet Experiment*, p. 245-256.

23 Suny, *Soviet Experiment*, p. 259.

24 Khlevniuk, *Stalin*, p. 116.

25 Jochen Hellbeck, *Revolution on My Mind: Writing a Diary Under Stalin* (Harvard University Press, 2009), p. 7.

26 Mark Edele, (Oxford University Press, 2008), pp. 2-3.

27 I. V. Stalin, 'Speech at the First All-Union Conference of Stakhanovites', November 17, 1935: http:// soviethistory.msu.edu/1936-2/ year-of-the-stakhanovite/ year-of-the-stakhanovite-texts/stalin-at-the-conference-of-stakhanovites/

28 Stephen Kotkin, *Magnetic Mountain: Stalinism as a Civilization* (University of California Press, 1997), p. 202.

29 Lynne Viola, *Peasant Rebels Under Stalin: Collectivization and the Culture of Peasant Resistance* (Oxford University Press, 1999), p. 239.

30 Lev Trotsky, *The Revolution Betrayed:* https://www.marxists.org/archive/trotsky/1936/revbet/ch09.htm

31 Kotkin, *Magnetic Mountain*, p. 220.

32 Hellbeck, *Revolution*, pp. 13-14.

33 Terry Martin, *The Affirmative Action Empire: Nations and Nationalism in the Soviet Union, 1923–1939* (Cornell University Press, 2001), p. 22.

34 Kotkin, *Magnetic Mountain*, p. 23.

35 Nikita Khrushchev, Speech to the XX Congress of the Communist Party: https://www.theguardian.com/theguardian/2007/apr/26/greatspeeches2.

36 Jan Plamper, *The Stalin Cult* (Yale University Press, 2012), p. 124.

37 Khlevniuk, *Stalin*, p. 149.

38 Khlevniuk, *Stalin*, p. 144.

39 Plamper, *Stalin Cult*, p. xiii.

40 Roy Medvedev, *Let History Judge: The Origins and Consequences of Stalinism*

1 Robert Service, *Stalin: A Biography* (Harvard University Press, 2008), p. 11.

2 Oleg V. Khlevniuk, *Stalin: New Biography of a Dictator*, trans. by Nora Seligman Favorov (Yale University Press, 2015), p. 12.

3 Isaac Deutscher, *Stalin: A Political Biography* (Oxford University Press, 1972), p. 23.

4 Stephen Kotkin, *Stalin, Vol. I: Paradoxes of Power, 1878-1928* (Penguin, 2014), p. 27.

5 Khlevniuk, *Stalin*, p. 12.

6 Service, *Stalin*, p. 58.

7 Ronald Suny, *The Soviet Experiment: Russia, the USSR, and the Successor States* (Oxford University Press, 2010), p. 72.

8 Laura Engelstein, *Russia in Flames: War, Revolution, Civil War, 1914 - 1921* (Oxford University Press, 2017), p. xviii.

9 Kotkin, *Stalin*, Vol. I, p. 301.

10 Service, *Stalin*, p. 4.

11 Khlevniuk, *Stalin*, p. 71.

12 Khlevniuk, *Stalin*, p. 56.

13 Simon Sebag Montefiore, *Young Stalin* (Weidenfeld & Nicolson, 2010), p. 218.

14 Khlevniuk, *Stalin*, p. 13.

15 Sebag Montefiore, *Young Stalin*, p. 251.

16 Khlevniuk, *Stalin*, p. 253.

17 Sebag Montefiore, *Stalin*, p. 198.

18 Sarah Davies and James Harris, *Stalin's World: Dictating the Soviet Order* (Yale University Press, 2014), p. 16.

19 Suny, *Soviet Experiment*, p. 254.

20 Khlevniuk, *Stalin*, p. 116.

21 I. V. Stalin, 'A Year of Great Change',

(Columbia University Press, 1990), p. 365.

41   Rupert Colley, *Stalin: History in an Hour* (HarperCollins UK, 2012), p. 1.

42   Sarah Davies, *Popular Opinion in Stalin's Russia: Terror, Propaganda and Dissent, 1934-1941* (Cambridge University Press, 1997), pp. 104-5.

43   Geoffrey Hosking, in Davies, *Popular Opinion*, p. 102.

44   Lewis Siegelbaum, 'Stalin Constitution': http://soviethistory.msu.edu/1936-2/stalin-constitution/

45   Serhy Yekelchyk, *Stalin's Citizens: Everyday Politics in the Wake of Total War* (Oxford University Press, 2014), p. 7.

46   David L. Hoffmann, *Stalinist Values: The Cultural Norms of Soviet Modernity, 1917-1941* (Cornell University Press, 2003), pp. 55-56.

47   Khlevniuk, *Stalin*, p. 147.

48   Khlevniuk, *Stalin*, p. 145.

49   Sheila Fitzpatrick, *On Stalin's Team: The Years of Living Dangerously in Soviet Politics* (Princeton University Press, 2015), p. 2.

50   Hellbeck, *Revolution*, p. 164.

51   Peter Holquist, 'State Violence as Technique: The Logic of Violence in Soviet Totalitarianism', in *Stalinism: The Essential Readings,* ed. David Hoffmann (Blackwell, 2003), pp. 133-134.

52   Katerina Clark, *Petersburg: Crucible of Cultural Revolution* (Harvard University Press, 2010), p. 296.

53   Kotkin, *Magnetic Mountain*, p. 21.

54   Kate Brown, 'Gridded Lives: Why Kazakhstan and Montana are Nearly the Same Place', T*he American Historical Review*, Vol. 106, No. 1 (Feb. 2001), pp. 17-48.

55   Martin Malia, *The Soviet Tragedy: A History of Socialism in Russia, 1917-1991* (Free Press, 1995), p. 178.

56   Sarah Davies, 'Stalin as Patron of Cinema: Creating Soviet Mass Culture, 1932-1936', in *Stalin: A New History, ed. Sarah Davies and James Harris* (Cambridge University Press, 2009), p. 219.

57   Khlevniuk, *Stalin*, p. 97

58   Yuri Slezkine, *The House of Government: A Saga of the Russian Revolution* (Princeton University Press, 2017), p. 475.

59   I. V. Stalin, 'Morning', translated by Donald Rayfield.

60   Donald Rayfield, 'Stalin as Poet', *PN Review*, Vol. 11, No. 3, January-February 1985

61   Rayfield, 'Stalin as Poet'.

62   Ethan Pollock, *Stalin and the Soviet Science Wars* (Princeton Oxford: Princeton University Press, 2008), p. 1.

63   Pollock, *Stalin*, p. 2.

64   Miriam Dobson, *Khrushchev's Cold Summer: Gulag Returnees, Crime, and the Fate of Reform after Stalin* (Cornell University Press, 2009), p. 134.

65   Suny, *Soviet Experiment*, p. 288.

66   J. Arch Getty and Oleg V. Naumov, *The Road to Terror*, trans. Benjamin Sher (Yale University Press, 2010), p. xiv.

67   James Harris, T*he Great Urals: Regionalism and the Evolution of the Soviet System* (Cornell University Press, 1999), p. 147.

68   Paul Hagenloh, 'Socially Harmful Elements and the Great Terror', in *Stalinism: New Directions,* ed. Sheila Fitzpatrick (Routledge, 1999), p. 286.

69   Hellbeck, *Revolution*, p. 35.

70   Steven A. Barnes, *Death and Redemption: The Gulag and the Shaping of Soviet Society* (Princeton University Press, 2011), p. 2.

71   Bogdan Musial, 'The "Polish Operation" of the NKVD: The Climax of the Terror Against the Polish Minority in the Soviet Union', *Journal of Contemporary History*, Vol. 48, No. 1 (2013), p. 109.

72   Malia, *Soviet Tragedy*, p. 179.

73   Khlevniuk, *Stalin*, p. 152.

74   Aleksandr Solzhenitsyn, *The Gulag Archipelago*, trans. Thomas P. Whitney and Harry Willets (Harvill Press, 2003), p. 74.

75   Nikolai Bukharin, Letter to Stalin, December 10, 1937, in *The Structure of*

Soviet History: Essays and Documents, ed. Ronald Grigor Suny (Oxford University Press, 2002), pp. 245-259.

76   V. M. Molotov, in Khlevniuk, *Stalin*, p. 156.

77   Timothy Snyder, *Bloodlands: Europe between Hitler and Stalin* (Vintage, 2011), p. 115.

78   Mark Harrison, in Suny, *Soviet Experiment*, p. 348.

79   Suny, *Soviet Experiment*, p. 320

80   Khlevniuk, *Stalin*, p. 238.

81   Elena Zubkova, *Russia After the War: Hopes, Illusions and Disappointments, 1945-1957* (Routledge, 1998), p. 32.

82   Service, *Stalin*, p. 491.

83   Khlevniuk, *Stalin*, p. 240.

84   Khlevniuk, *Stalin*, p. 197.

85   Juliane Fürst, '*Introduction*', in *Late Stalinist Russia: Society Between Reconstruction and Reinvention*, ed. by (Routledge, 2009), p. 2.

86   Fürst, 'Introduction', p. 9.

87   Christopher Read, *Stalin: From the Caucasus to the Kremlin* (Routledge, 2016), p. 308.

88   Polly Jones, *Myth, Memory, Trauma: Rethinking the Stalinist Past in the Soviet Union, 1953-70* (Yale University Press, 2013), p. 110.

89   Dobson, *Khrushchev's Cold Summer*, p. 6.

90   Evgenii Evtushenko, 'Stalin's Heirs': http://soviethistory.msu.edu/1961-2/thaw-poets/thaw-poets-texts/evtushenko-on-stalins-heirs/

91   Medvedev, *Let History Judge*, p. 566.

92   Abram Terz (Andrei Siniavskii), *The Trial Begins, and, On Socialist Realism* (University of California Press, 1992), p. 141.

93   Kathleen E. Smith, *Remembering Stalin's Victims: Popular Memory and the End of the USSR* (Cornell University Press, 1996), p. 45.

94   Rosalind Marsh, *Literature, History and Identity in Post-Soviet Russia, 1991-2006* (Peter Lang, 2007), p. 450.

95   Maria Lipman, 'Stalin Is Not Dead: A Legacy that Holds Back Russia', in *The Stalin Puzzle: Deciphering Post-Soviet Public Opinion* (Carnegie Endowment for International Peace, 2013), p. 22.

96   Khlevniuk, *Stalin*, p. x

INDEX